CO-ASR-464

HOW TO MAKE MONEY
INVESTING ABROAD

HOW TO MAKE MONEY INVESTING ABROAD

TAKING ADVANTAGE OF NEW OPPORTUNITIES IN THE GLOBAL MARKETPLACE

Nancy Dunnan and Douglas Schaff

HarperCollins*Publishers*

HarperCollins books may be purchased for educational, business, or sales promotional use. For information, please write to: Special Markets Department, HarperCollins Publishers, Inc., 10 East 53rd Street, New York, N.Y. 10022.

FIRST EDITION

Book design Maura Fadden Rosenthal

Illustrations by Irving Perkins Associates, Inc.

Maps by Paul Pugliese

Library of Congress Cataloging-in-Publication Data
Dunnan, Nancy.
    How to make money investing abroad / Nancy Dunnan and Douglas Schaff. — 1st ed.
        p.   cm.
    Includes index.

    ISBN 0-06-270112-6
    1. Investments. Foreign—Handbooks, manuals, etc. 2. Success in business—Handbooks, manuals, etc. I. Schaff, Douglas, 1952–   .
II. Title
HG4538.D816 1994
332.6'7314—dc20   94-4739

94 95 96 97 98 ❖/RRD 10 9 8 7 6 5 4 3 2 1

To Terry, Ian, Andrew and Erin Schaff,

and Jay J. Pack

This book would not have been written without the tireless assistance of
Terry Schaff and research expertise of Jay Pack.
In addition we wish to thank Shirley Roth.
And, special thanks to Joseph Spieler, our agent,
and Robert Wilson, our editor at HarperCollins.

CONTENTS

PART V: OTHER GLOBAL OPPORTUNITIES

APPENDIX

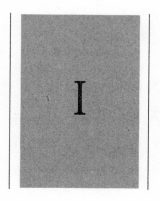

BEGINNING STEPS

CHAPTER ONE

WHY INVEST ABROAD?

Investing worldwide can increase your profits and lower the overall risk of your portfolio. Too good to be true? A study of world markets between 1977 and 1991[1] showed that an investment portfolio composed of 60 percent U.S. equities and 40 percent foreign equities was less risky than a portfolio composed solely of U.S. stocks, and that a global portfolio earned on average 2.2 percent more each year than a U.S.-only portfolio.

How is this possible? A key reason for the decreased risk is that each country, though a member of the global community, still operates on its own economic cycle. So while one country's stock market is nearing the end of its bull market, another country's is just getting started. The result is more stable returns for portfolios that include investments in different countries. International diversification should be of particular benefit in the next few years; with Wall Street's bull market having passed the decade marker, dollar interest rates hitting rock bottom, and taxes going up, it is unlikely that U.S. stocks and bonds will keep pace with the performance of foreign markets.

---

1. From a study done by Morgan Stanley Capital International.

Although there are plenty of investment opportunities in the United States, many of the world's fastest-growing economies are overseas; therefore, foreign markets should be included in the universe of investment possibilities you consider.

DRAMATIC GROWTH ABROAD

Over the past decade, foreign markets have grown to represent two-thirds of the world's total stock market value.
In the past decade, robust economic growth propelled many foreign markets ahead of the United States.

THE WORLD STAGE: A PLATFORM FOR PROFITS

From the collapse of the Berlin Wall to the Trade Agreement with the United States, Mexico, and Canada, sweeping politi-

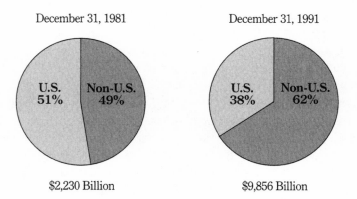

GLOBAL MARKETS INCREASE OPPORTUNITY
World Stock Market Capitalization

December 31, 1981   December 31, 1991

U.S. 51%   Non-U.S. 49%   U.S. 38%   Non-U.S. 62%

$2,230 Billion $9,856 Billion

SOURCE: Morgan Stanley Capital International

WORLD STOCK MARKETS

Average Annual Returns for 10 Years Ended 12/31/92

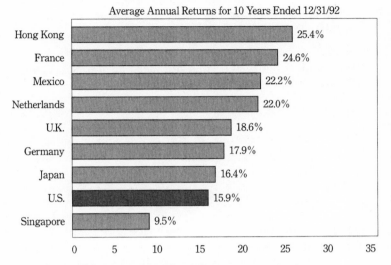

Hong Kong	25.4%
France	24.6%
Mexico	22.2%
Netherlands	22.0%
U.K.	18.6%
Germany	17.9%
Japan	16.4%
U.S.	15.9%
Singapore	9.5%

SOURCE: Morgan Stanley Capital International
Returns are measured in U.S. currency and should not be considered representative of an investment in any fund. Past performance is not indicative of future results.

cal and economic changes are creating an environment for dramatic economic growth. Consider:

- Throughout the world, governments are selling off state-controlled companies to individual and corporate investors. These "privatizations" will accelerate in the 1990s, liberating capital, entrepreneurial ventures, and consequent economic development.

- A democratic tide has swept away most Latin American dictatorships, allowing new administrations to negotiate breakthrough debt-restructuring agreements, with the result that the *Latin American debt burden is significantly lower today than it was five years ago*.

- Pro-business government policies and low labor costs are increasing trade volumes in southeast Asia.

- Modern telecommunications allow capital to flow instantaneously across borders, and multinational companies to compete globally for resources and markets.

- Trade barriers within western Europe have been removed, creating a marketplace larger than the United States.

- Tariffs have been reduced or eliminated among Canada, Mexico, and the United States, creating the largest free-trade zone in the world and stimulating investments, jobs, and trade.

MECHANICS AND GUIDELINES

This is an opportune time to master the guidelines for successfully investing in foreign markets. The essential mechanics that we provide can be learned and put into practice by anyone with the time and interest to do so. As a first step, we will look at the key differences between investing in the United States and investing abroad.

UNDERSTANDING THE RISKS

Investing overseas carries the same risks as owning American stocks and bonds, but with some special considerations.

CURRENCY FLUCTUATIONS

Changes in the value of a foreign currency add a potential profit or loss:

- The price of a foreign stock will rise (or fall) in its local currency.

- The value of that country's currency can go up (or down) versus the U.S. dollar, thereby increasing or decreasing the value of your foreign stock.

1

THE FLUCTUATING DOLLAR AND YOUR FOREIGN INVESTMENTS

Say an investor pays 10 British pounds (£) each for one hundred shares of Unilever Ltd. on London's International Stock Exchange, on a day when one pound was worth $1.50.

> Total cost in £: 100 shares at £10 each =£1,000
> How many dollars did the investor pay?
> £1,000 x $1.50 each = $1,500

Where the pound is priced against the dollar three months hence could significantly affect the U.S. dollar value of the one hundred shares of Unilever, even if the share price remains the same.

If, three months later, the pound has gone up to $1.75, then the investment is worth (100 x £10) x $1.75 =$1,750, for a *Net Currency Gain* of +16.7 percent.

At start: £1.00 = $1.50 and the one hundred shares are worth $1,500.

But if, three months later, the pound has fallen to $1.25, then the investment is worth (100 x £10) x $1.25= $1,250, for a *Net Currency Loss* of -16.7 percent.

The strongest position to be in is when you own a foreign stock that is increasing in price at the same time as the country's currency is rising against the dollar. For example, in the first half of 1993, funds heavily invested in Japanese stocks rose nearly 35 percent, aided by currency gains roughly equaling those of the stocks themselves. In fact, the Japanese yen has been appreciating against the dollar since 1985, increasing the overall returns to U.S. investors who had been holding Japanese securities. However, there is no guarantee that such trends will continue. Should the yen decline relative to the dollar, that would lower returns on Japanese securities for U.S. investors. Chapter 12 is devoted to helping ensure that foreign currencies work for, not against, you.

> *Note*: You do not have to buy foreign currency in order to invest abroad. Chapters 3, 4, and 5 will show you how to invest in foreign companies without having to convert your dollars into another currency.

Further, the currency portion of some foreign investments can be partially or fully hedged by a market professional. (See Part Three.)

LIMITED INFORMATION

Major newspapers now regularly report closing prices on a wide selection of foreign stocks. Although there is generally less publicly accessible information on foreign companies than is typical of U.S. businesses, this situation is improving as more data become available from overseas markets and as more stock analysts in the United States become familiar with those markets. A number of U.S. banks and brokerage houses produce excellent research reports on foreign companies, and you can obtain them. Expect a slew of information in the coming years from overseas governments as they sell state-controlled businesses—British Rail, Air France, Italy's giant ENI holding company, and Germany's Deutsche Telekom, to name a few. Investment bankers estimate that more than $30 billion of such "privatizations" will occur annually throughout the 1990s, much of it aimed at U.S. investors and markets.

Costs

The expense of buying and selling foreign securities is higher than with U.S. stocks and bonds. Though mutual funds can be an efficient way to invest abroad, a thorough reading of any international fund prospectus is a must. Watch the ratio of expenses to assets under management, which runs higher, on average, for overseas funds. For 274 international equity funds in 1994, the average expense ratio was 1.8 percent, versus 1.4 percent for domestic growth funds and 1.2 percent for domestic growth and income funds.

> *Note*: Of ten top-ranked international funds, only two had expenses higher than the average. Front-end sales fees differ dramatically by more than 5 percent for funds specializing in the same region—the Far East, for example. International no-load funds do exist, and we will tell you about them in Chapters 7 and 10.

Less Supervision of Foreign Stock Exchanges

From Bangkok to Buenos Aires, foreign regulators are getting better organized and making their markets more accessible to global investors. Don't expect, though, to find versions of the U.S. Securities and Exchange Commission overseeing the smaller foreign markets anytime soon. It is more difficult to obtain and enforce judgments against foreign companies and brokers than those based in the U.S., so invest only through a brokerage firm with a solid reputation. See Appendix.

Different Accounting Rules

Foreign corporations are often not subject to uniform accounting, auditing, and financial reporting standards. The best strategy is to rely on the investment reports of a firm that has an analyst whose specialty is interpreting international statements, or to purchase ADRs.

Less Liquidity

The average trading volume for some foreign securities is relatively small, with the result that their individual prices are more volatile than those of U.S. companies. Additionally, if the market is thin when you want to sell, you may not get as good a price as you are used to on U.S. stocks.

Coups and Volcanoes

You cannot rule out the prospect of political instability, even in countries that have made economic reforms and are reaping the benefits. Estimates are that 200 million Chinese will lift themselves to the middle class by the second half of the 1990s, up from 60 million in 1990. Political brinkmanship may accompany economic change as calls for fewer government directives becomes stronger, such as China's forced purchase of its bonds in 1993. While the bond purchase effectively reduced the money supply and moderated economic growth and inflation, it was detested by the Chinese businesses forced to buy the bonds, because (among other reasons) the government paid just half the prevailing rate of interest. An important rule, however, is not to sell on the basis of political rumors. In Hong Kong, for example, the stock market has appreciated based on the assumption that the 1997 Chinese takeover of the colony will leave intact Hong Kong's *laissez-faire* capitalism. Breaks in the market, based on events countering the smooth-takeover assumption, have been short-lived. Such dips in foreign markets, against the grain of longer-term economic interest, should generally, over the next five years, be used as opportunities to buy equities at cheaper prices. That being true, the best insurance against the return of centralized economic planning will be the rising per capita income of foreign populations.

You're Not in Kansas

In extreme situations, a foreign government can change the rules of the game entirely: expropriate a company; nationalize it; introduce currency controls, making it more difficult to bring your money home; or introduce confiscatory taxes. (Clearly, there is small chance of such disruption in Britain, Switzerland, Japan, and other countries with established markets.) Such extreme action would work against the self-interest of the country instigating it by cutting off needed financing and isolating it from international sources of capital. But in the past some governments have ignored this consequence and shot themselves in the foot. Take Brazil, for example: In the 1970s, banks and international lending organizations lent it tens of billions of dollars, and its economy soared. The 1980s, however, began with a deep recession, and then came the spectacular crisis in 1982, when the country reneged on paying its debt. It took the rest of the decade for our major banks to recover from massive write-downs on Brazilian debt. Devoid of credit, Brazil's economy reeled in and out of recession while its annual inflation rate flew into the thousands.

Global trends are in the other direction, however—toward cooperation and strengthening of institutions that protect foreign investors. This is due in part to the increasing foreign investment of U.S. pension and mutual funds. In fact, pension funds plan to boost their holdings of international bonds and equities during the 1990s by 500 percent.

Six Reasons Foreign Investing Will Be Profitable in the 1990s

- *Opportunity*: More than 60 percent of the world's listed stocks and fixed-income securities are outside the United States. Many stocks have been outstanding winners. Others are bound to be. Ten of our major trading partners are paying higher interest rates than we are, sometimes twice the U.S. rate on CDs, money market funds, and bonds. We will lay out the full range of foreign investments to choose from, where to find them, when to buy them, and when to get out.

- *Growth*: Many newly industrialized countries will continue to expand at rates two to three times faster than the United States. China's economy, for example, grew at a sizzling 13 percent in 1993 and almost as much in 1994. Even utility companies in such countries are growth stocks. We will tell you which countries to invest in now and which investments will be the most profitable, whether real estate, stocks, bonds, or currencies.
- *Industry Leadership:* Foreign countries dominate certain industries, such as:

Consumer electronics: Japan
Heavy machinery: Germany
Low-priced manufactured goods: Asia

To participate in the growth phase of such industries, you will need to know about the foreign companies involved in these areas. We will tell you about them and their "American Depositary Receipts" (ADRs), stock equivalents priced in dollars and traded on U.S. exchanges.

- *Diversification:* The world's economies are in different phases of the business cycle. Right now, Germany and Japan are at the start of their growth cycle, while the United States and many Latin American countries are in the midst of theirs. A diversified global investment program will provide portfolio appreciation and reduce risk. One's investments should never be entirely in one basket—or in one country.
- *Protection against the dollar*: The U.S. dollar moves up and down continually against other currencies. Investing a portion of your portfolio in foreign curren-

cies makes sense, but many investors are put off by the seemingly complex notion of currency risk, which they consider the domain of Wall Street professionals. We will dispel that myth and show how to invest in other currencies for profit and to protect against severe economic shocks at home.

- *Pension fund buying*: To meet their targets, these investment leviathans will have to buy at least $40 billion worth of foreign stocks and bonds every year. Compare that with their 1990 total holdings of $70 billion, and you can see why setbacks in foreign markets will be looked at as buying opportunities. When you buy foreign, you will not be buying alone.

CHAPTER TWO

BEFORE YOU START

Now that you're convinced of the importance of investing outside the United States, you're faced with deciding when, where, and how much.

Wise investing abroad is very much the same as wise investing on Wall Street. In both cases, before you begin you must address these three key points:

1) Can I afford to invest in the market?
2) Am I investing for growth or income, or both?
3) What is my tolerance for risk?

Let's take a moment to look at all three.

First, you have no business putting money into foreign markets unless you have accumulated sufficient cash to support yourself and your family through an emergency, such as being out of work or handling a serious illness. Conventional wisdom: Have at least six (preferably nine) months' of living costs in a liquid investment.

Second, once you decide to invest, know beforehand if you want appreciation or income—or a combination of the two. It seems like a simple distinction, but many sophisticated investors often lose sight of their investment objectives and complain when a stock has a low yield or a fixed-income vehicle moves up very little or not at all in price.

Third, think about how much risk you can or should tolerate. The rule of thumb: The higher the yield or potential for appreciation, the higher the risk. Junk bonds have higher yields than Treasuries, and for a good reason: They are less safe than T-bills and bonds, which are backed by the U.S. government. The late Harold L. Rosenthal, a well-recognized bond expert and founder of a succesful Wall Street firm, developed a simple but ideal approach to risk: "Invest to, but not beyond, the point where you can sleep comfortably."

The two pyramids in the accompanying illustration will give you a good fix on the risk levels of most U.S. and foreign investments. You should also factor in your age and family responsibilities in building a portfolio. People in retirement generally need more current income from investments than those drawing a salary. Younger people with few familiy responsibilities can opt for more growth in their choices, as can parents setting up an education fund for their children.

We'll look at the different levels on both pyramids, starting with the lowest risk level (Level 1) and moving up to Level 4 at the peak of the pyramid, where the risk factor is highest.

THE DOMESTIC PYRAMID

LEVEL 1

Level 1 covers your basic financial needs and consists of the emergency nest egg we just discussed. Your nest egg should be in safe, liquid investments that pay interest, such as certificates of deposit and money market funds. Level 1 also includes health, life and disability insurance, your retirement plan, and your IRA, Keogh, or SEP.

Do not leave Level 1 until you have covered these basic needs.

DOMESTIC INVESTMENT PYRAMID

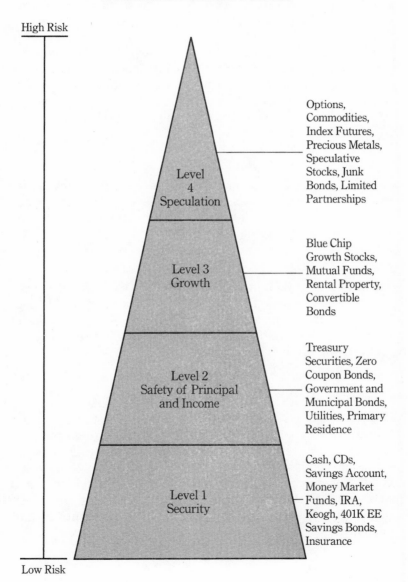

High Risk

Level
4
Speculation

Options,
Commodities,
Index Futures,
Precious Metals,
Speculative
Stocks, Junk
Bonds, Limited
Partnerships

Level 3
Growth

Blue Chip
Growth Stocks,
Mutual Funds,
Rental Property,
Convertible
Bonds

Level 2
Safety of Principal
and Income

Treasury
Securities, Zero
Coupon Bonds,
Government and
Municipal Bonds,
Utilities, Primary
Residence

Level 1
Security

Cash, CDs,
Savings Account,
Money Market
Funds, IRA,
Keogh, 401K EE
Savings Bonds,
Insurance

Low Risk

LEVEL 2

On Level 2 you will find safe, income-producing choices such as high-rated corporate and municipal bonds, U.S. Treasury bills, notes and bonds, zero coupon bonds, and real estate— that is, your primary residence. These investments, slightly higher in risk than those in Level 1, are accompanied by higher yields. Zero coupon bonds, CDs, and longer-term Treasuries can be timed to mature at a certain date and are an excellent way to meet staggering college tuition and retirement costs.

LEVEL 3

At this point you're financially secure enough to invest for growth. Blue-chip stocks, growth stocks, and mutual funds that invest in both of these, as well as index funds are good choices, along with rental property.

LEVEL 4

The pinnacle of the pyramid is devoted to the riskiest investments, which, if you pick well *and* are lucky, may yield spectacular returns. These include speculative stocks, stocks in new companies, options, commodities, index futures, gold and precious metals, and junk bonds.

THE FOREIGN PYRAMID

Now let's look at an investment pyramid devoted to foreign securities. Our advice: Don't move into the foreign pyramid until you are at least halfway up Level 2 of the domestic pyramid. Although you will find similar types of investments—stocks, bonds, government issues, mutual funds, closed-end funds, and so on—in both pyramids, those in the foreign pyramid are subject to currency risk, something domestic investments do not encounter.

INTERNATIONAL INVESTMENT PYRAMID

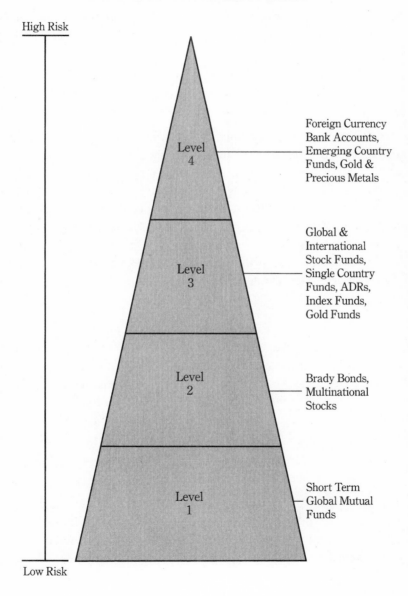

High Risk

Level 4 — Foreign Currency Bank Accounts, Emerging Country Funds, Gold & Precious Metals

Level 3 — Global & International Stock Funds, Single Country Funds, ADRs, Index Funds, Gold Funds

Level 2 — Brady Bonds, Multinational Stocks

Level 1 — Short Term Global Mutual Funds

Low Risk

LEVEL 1

Although there is no low-risk foreign investment that exactly parallels EE savings bonds, FDIC-insured CDs, and money market funds, short-term global bond funds, described in Chapter 7 and the Appendix, are the closest thing. Again, we remind you that these funds can be negatively influenced by currency swings.

LEVEL 2

Brady bonds, which are backed by U.S. Treasury bonds, and conservative foreign bond funds are appropriate investments at this level. Bear in mind that these longer-term bonds are placed on Level 2 because they fluctuate more in price than short-term global funds. Brady bonds are covered in Chapter 5 and bond funds in Chapter 7. Stocks in multinational corporations (those that have significant foreign operations) are one way to armchair invest in overseas markets without too much risk. Chapter 4 lists suggested multinationals.

LEVEL 3

By now you have gained a greater grasp of the foreign markets and can consider global and international stock funds as well as single country funds of politically stable countries. See Part 4. If you wish to select individual foreign stocks, look to ADRs, covered in Chapter 3. European and Asian index funds mirror those markets and are explained in Chapter 10.

LEVEL 4

Emerging-country mutual funds and closed-end funds in Chapters 8 and 9, foreign currencies in Chapter 12 as well as foreign-currency bank accounts (Appendix) may reward you with spectacular returns or, at times, with serious losses.

GATHERING INFORMATION

Throughout this book you will find background information along with specific stock and mutual-fund suggestions to help in assembling your foreign investment pyramid. In particular, review the mutual-fund and stock picks in each of the 25 Country Spotlights. The three individual portfolios, arranged by risk level and laid out in the Appendix, can be used as basic models and then tailored to accommodate your particular "sleeping level."

We also recommend that you choose a leading publication, subscribe so you will have it in house at all times, and then actually read it. A list of suggested publications with their toll-free numbers is given in the Appendix. One of our favorites is *The Economist*. In 1994, this weekly magazine, published in London but readily available in the United States, began regular coverage of twenty-four emerging markets and fifteen OECD countries. The information is arranged so you can see at a glance what is happening to interest rates and stock markets in each of these countries.

Perhaps even more useful is the magazine's "Portfolio Poll" of big fund managers, which tracks where these professionals are putting their money. Those polled are: Merrill Lynch, Lehman Brothers, Nikko Securities, Daiwa Europe, Credit Agricole, Robeco Group Asset Management, Bank Julius Baer (Zurich), UBS International Investment, Commerz International Capital Management, and Credit Suisse Asset Management.

In the January 15, 1994 issue, for example, you would have learned that portfolio managers were beginning the year cautiously, cutting back equity positions from 54 percent to 52 percent and bonds from from 41 percent to under 40 percent. One manager, Lehman Brothers, moved 5 percent of its assets into gold. The percentage of holdings managers have in each individual country, including the United States, Britain,

Germany, France, and other European countries, as well as Japan and the Far Eastern countries, is given. A separate table shows their bond holdings by type of currency.

If you find that selecting securities is too time-consuming or "not your thing," you can easily participate in "off Wall Street" markets through mutual funds—where the decision making is left to the pros. Part 3 is entirely devoted to the different types of open and closed-end funds and the top performers in each category, country, or region.

So, pick and choose carefully among the various investment choices presented in the following chapters, remembering the adage "What goes up must come down." Translated into money management, that means: Don't be greedy, and remember to take profits from time to time.

A final thought to keep in mind as you develop and fine-tune your foreign investment portfolio comes from the CEO of Berkshire Hathaway, Warren Buffet: "Should you find yourself in a chronically leaking boat, energy devoted to changing vessels is likely to be more productive than energy devoted to patching leaks."

II

GOING GLOBAL WITHOUT
LEAVING THE DOLLAR

CHAPTER THREE

AMERICAN DEPOSITARY RECEIPTS

During 1993, shares of **Telebras**, the Brazilian telephone company, jumped nearly 300 percent in price. Between 1992 and the end of 1993, shares of **Advanced Info Services**, a Thai firm, rose about 250 percent; and **Danka Business Systems**, a U.K. company, saw a 400 percent increase. What do these three stocks have in common in addition to their soaring prices? They all trade in the United States as ADRs, or American Depositary Receipts. One of the easiest ways for investors living in the United States to participate directly in foreign stocks is through American Depositary Receipts, commonly known as ADRs, or sometimes as ADS, the S standing for shares. These are negotiable securities representing ownership of stock of a foreign company.

ADRs are issued by U.S. banks against the actual shares of a foreign company. These foreign shares are in turn held in a custodial account by a branch or correspondent institution overseas, in the company's home country. The bank receives any dividends the company pays, converts them into dollars, and passes them onto the ADR investor. It also withholds taxes and provides annual and quarterly reports and other materials in English. ADRs trade just like U.S.

stocks and are bought and sold through full-service and discount stockbrokers.

Today, 1,143 companies, from huge British Airways to the
little Belize Holdings, Inc., list ADRs, nearly twice the number listed in 1987. Enthusiasm for ADRs continues to grow: In
the past three years, more than 120 foreign companies have
listed their stock in the United States. That's almost $100 bil-
lion of securities registered with the SEC. **Glaxo Holdings**
PLC, the British pharmaceutical maker, became the New York
Stock Exchange's most active issue in 1992, the first foreign
listing to do so.

These 1,143 ADRs represent 50 or so countries, and,
according to "The ADR Universe," an annual compilation of all
active ADRs prepared by Bankers Trust, 256 are listed on the
exchanges or on NASDAQ. The remaining, about 75 percent,
are listed in the "pink sheets," the non-NASDAQ over-the-
counter market, with several trading privately. The largest
issuer is the Bank of New York, which traces its origins back
to Alexander Hamilton, our first Secretary of the Treasury.
Other leading depositories are Citibank and J. P. Morgan. The
U.K. leads the ADR list with 254, followed by Australia with
196, Japan with 156, South Africa with 92, Mexico with 44,
Hong Kong with 40, France with 31, Germany with 25 and
Italy with 26.

ADRs are bought and sold through stockbrokers.

TYPES OF ADRs: SPONSORED VERSUS UNSPONSORED

Not all ADRs are created equal. In fact, they come in two flavors: sponsored and unsponsored. The distinction is important
to investors. If an ADR is sponsored, the foreign company is
directly involved in the process and in fact, initiates it, beginning with appointing a bank to serve as the depositary for its
shares and to service its ADR holders. The foreign company
also absorbs most of the costs involved.

The advantage to the foreign company? ADRs provide a larger and more diversified shareholder base, new sources of capital, and wider, international product or service recognition—which translates into increased sales.

Only sponsored ADRs may be listed on the New York and American stock exchanges.

Note: The SEC requires American companies to comply with the Securities Act of 1933—specifically to provide full and fair disclosure of the character of securities sold in U.S. markets. Sponsored or listed ADRs meet most SEC disclosure requirements, which means that information on these ADRs must be made available to the public. Holders of sponsored ADRs have the right to vote by proxy on certain company matters and to receive the company's financial reports.

Among the popular sponsored ADRs are **Sony, Hitachi, British Airways, British Telecom**, and **Honda**.

Unsponsored ADRs, on the other hand, are created in response to general or perceived investor demand. The foreign company approves the creation of ADRs for its stock but does not jump in and get actively involved in the process. Instead, a bank or broker, acting on its own behalf, after determining that there's enough interest among American investors to go to the trouble and expense, purchases a certain number of the foreign company's shares and puts them in trust. Any number of banks can serve as depositaries for unsponsored ADRs. The bank, not the company, pays the related expenses and acts both as depositary and issuer. These unsponsored ADRs are offered with minimal SEC compliance and reporting. The only SEC requirement is that financial disclosure available in the company's home country be made available to U.S. investors. Does the difference really matter? Yes. Because the foreign company is not directly involved in an unsponsored ADR, the bank is regarded as the owner of the shares, and although investors have the right to receive dividends (which will be in dollars), the bank has all voting rights. But more important, administration costs for an unsponsored ADR are borne by the investor—typically deducted from dividend payouts, which can cut dividends by several cents. (With a sponsored ADR the investor bears no costs except a broker's commission for buying and selling.) And, in most cases, with an unsponsored ADR, the annual report, proxy statements, and other company information are not given to the investor.

1

INVESTOR CAUTION

Three ADRs in four, including almost all of the unsponsored ones, are offered over the counter on pink sheets published daily by the National Quotation Bureau. This is a listing of stocks trading outside the three major U.S. markets. Because the New York Stock Exchange, the American Stock Exchange, and NASDAQ (National Association of Securities Dealers Automated Quotation system) require SEC disclosure for ADRs that is similar to disclosure requirements for U.S. stocks, unsponsored ADRs are limited to the pink sheets, and they need only follow their home country's accounting and disclosure practices. The exception: a handful of older ADRs that have been grandfathered on one of the major markets.

Caution: Unless you are an experienced ADR trader, stick with sponsored, listed issues for which much more information is available.

MORE ON SEC DISCLOSURE

Investing in ADRs can be full of surprises. Take **Daimler-Benz**, for example. When this huge German industrial corporation listed its stock on the New York Stock Exchange in September 1993, it published two very different stories about its first six months' finances. To the Germany investor, Daimler said it had earned $99 million; to its U.S. investors, it revealed a $558 million loss. Why the striking difference? German accounting regulations allow companies to smooth earnings by establishing reserves in good years and drawing upon these reserves in poor years. Daimler could not use hidden reserves when reporting to ADR holders.

Richard Breeden, chairman of the SEC, said this about the situation: "Under the German accounting system, a company decides what earnings it wants to report...[and it] can be reporting consistent growth...when profits could be falling....A small group of insiders know the truth, and they are free to trade against the public."

U.S. disclosure rules, however, are the strictest in the world, and they were put into place to protect American investors—to let them compare key results of foreign companies traded in this country with those of U.S.-based companies.

Value Line Investment Survey follows about 150 foreign American Depositary Receipts and Canadian stocks traded in the United States. The SEC requires all but a few to report their financial results according to U.S. or Canadian GAAP (Generally Accepted Accounting Procedures). The exceptions are based on the SEC's grandfather rule for stocks that traded in the U.S. before the adoption of the GAAP regulation.

THE ADVANTAGES OF ADRs

There are some very real advantages to buying ADRs instead of foreign stocks. With foreign stocks, it's often difficult to know the price at which the shares are quoted, when dividends are paid, and when stockholders meetings are held. Unlike registered U.S. securities, most foreign stocks are issued in bearer form. The investor is required to submit coupons for dividends and, when selling shares, physically deliver the security to the purchaser.

Furthermore, many brokerage firms do not handle nondollar denominated assets, and those that do usually require relatively large minimum investments for buying shares on a foreign exchange. ADRs, however, can be bought in small amounts. And the U.K., Japan, and Australia, which are major suppliers of ADRs, have actually signed treaties with the United States to simplify the tax treatment of dividends.

Other factors that add to their appeal:

1) You avoid the expense, red tape, and general hassle of buying stocks on a foreign exchange.

2) The ADR is denominated and quoted in U.S. dollars and trades just like a U.S. stock.

3) ADRs, particularly sponsored ones, tend to be of blue-chip quality—a foreign company will go through the lengthy process and expense of setting up an ADR program and subjecting itself to SEC disclosure requirements only if it is solidly positioned and intent upon having U.S. investors.

4) Stockbroker commissions are considerabaly smaller than would be charged if you bought the same securities on foreign markets.

5) Transactions are typically settled within five days, whereas on some foreign exchanges, settlement can take two weeks, even longer. And,

6) Dividends, of course, are paid in dollars.

WHICH TYPE OF ADR TO BUY

If you are new to the world of global investing, you would do well to stick with ADRs listed on the New York or American stock exchanges or on NASDAQ. However, your choice is somewhat limited. Of the 26 percent of all ADRs listed, about

11 percent are on the New York Stock Exchange, 9 percent on NASDAQ and under 1 percent on the American Stock Exchange. The remaining 5 percent are in private placements.

In fact, unsponsored ADRs that trade in the pink sheet market are often illiquid, and at times they are difficult to buy or sell. And, further complicating matters, pink sheet prices are not published in newspapers but are supplied by traders, who determine the price based on their own supply, demand, and perceptions of risk.

THE CURRENCY RISK FACTOR

Despite all their advantages, ADRs are not entirely risk-free. Although they are dollar denominated, their values will fluctuate along with foreign exchange rates. In fact, the market value of an ADR reflects the current rate of exchange between the foreign country and the United States. This exchange rate can work toward your advantage or not. If the dollar drops, for example, the value of your overseas investment increases. If the dollar goes up, the foreign investment is worth less.

Rule of thumb: An ADR can do better than the underlying stock if the dollar weakens and worse if the dollar strengthens.

When local currencies strengthen against the dollar, the return on the ADR is increased. So, if you own shares of an ADR in a country whose stock market is rising and whose currency is strengthening against the dollar, you're getting a double boost. Conversely, if the dollar is rising against the foreign currency, your ADR will suffer. Adding to your risk factor: Daily currency rate fluctuations are factored into the price of an ADR. For example, the debate over the fate of the North American Free Trade Agreement (NAFTA) in the fall of 1993 caused the Mexican peso to decline against the dollar. Because the weaker peso bought fewer dollars, ADRs on Mexican stocks lost value during that period.

The currency factor is very important in the short term, less so if you invest long term. Therefore, unless you want to try to outsmart currency moves, select ADRs as you would any domestic stock, on the basis of sound fundamentals: Is the company well run? Are earnings and revenues increasing? Is the product or service well received? Can the company cover its dividend and even raise it? In addition, you must factor in the political and economic condition and status of the country. (See Part 4.)

THE DISADVANTAGES OF ADRS

ADRs make trading in foreign securities easy, but keep in mind that mutual funds holding foreign stocks in their portfolios provide greater and usually safer access to global markets. The trading "environment" underlying foreign stocks is often very different from the environment in which U.S. stocks are traded. You may not know about adverse developments in a foreign country in time to react and protect your investment. On the other hand, mutual-fund managers are in touch with foreign markets on a minute-by-minute basis and also can use sophisticated hedging techniques to offset currency fluctuations. There are other factors to consider when buying ADRs. Depending upon the type of ADR, information can be spotty. Banks serving as depositaries often retain part of the dividend payments, may take a cut of currency translations, may charge for issuing ADR certificates, and may round off share prices to their advantage of buy-and-sell trades.

TAXES

Dividends on ADRs may be reduced by foreign withholding taxes. However, U.S. investors receive a full credit for these foreign taxes when they file their annual income-tax returns.

How to Buy ADRs

Before you begin investing, you should know that one ADR does not necessarily mean one share of stock. An ADR may represent one to ten shares of a company's foreign stock, so ask before you buy. The number of shares represented is determined when the trust is established and the ADRs are first issued.

Most investors who buy ADRs have them held in street name with their broker, just because it's easier. However, you can ask that you receive a certificate. Spreading your portfolio among several foreign markets—some of which will be moving up, others dropping—reduces your overall risk.

For More Information

Brokers specializing in foreign stocks can supply some research on most ADRs. And you can do some fairly sophisticated research on your own: *Value Line Investment Survey* (Phone: (800) 634-3583) and Standard & Poor's *The Outlook* (Phone: (212) 208-8000), two independent weekly research services, cover selected ADRs and recommend when to buy, hold, or sell individual issues. Both *The Outlook* and *Value Line* are available at large public libraries and brokerage firms. You can also subscribe to them. Call for current subscription prices.

Standard & Poor's Corporation issues "S&P Research Reports" on 120 ADRs. Those with three to five stars in the S&P ranking system indicate that the company's analysts expect superior market performance for these companies over the next twelve months. (See box.)

Your broker should be able to send you copies of these reports, or you can order them directly from Standard & Poor's by calling (800) 642-2858 from 8:00 A.M. to 9:00 P.M. eastern time, Monday through Friday. Each report costs $10, and the fee can be placed on MasterCard or VISA. They are mailed first class. For an additional charge "S&P Research Reports" can be sent via fax or overnight courier.

2

SPONSORED ADRS & ADS WITH S&P STARS

Company	Stars	Symbol	Price	Yield

British Airways   3   BAB $63   2.3%
One of the world's largest airlines; expanding global coverage through investments in foreign airlines; operations with USAir, increasing U.S. traffic.

British Gas   3   BRG $45   4.9%
Expansion of business outside U.K. should increase earnings.

Elf Acquitaine   3   ELF $38   2.9%
Rising production of crude oil and natural gas production should offset any weak European markets; company is strong in West Africa.

Glaxo Holdings plc 3   GLX $19   3.6%
One of the world's largest pharmaceutical companies, it has a long-term patent on Zantac, the anti-ulcer drug; also, many of its new products bode well for earnings.

Grand Metropolitan 3   GRM $26   2.9%
British-based consumer products company that has downsized and cut costs to improve profitability; holdings include Pillsbury, Green Giant, Smirnoff Vodka, Bailey's Original Irish Cream, and Burger King.

Hanson plc   4   HAN $20   5.7%
Conglomerate headquartered in U.K. has home-building, chemical, and coal-production divisions that should see upturns as U.S. and European economies rebound.

Imperial Chemical 3   ICI $51   3.4%
Major cost reductions will boost company's earnings.

News Corp   5   NWS $53   0.3%
Strong double-digit earnings gains expected to continue because of profits from major publishing and broadcasing operations in the United States, Australia, and the Middle East and Asia.

Orbital Engine   5   OE $13   —
Australia-based developer of clean-burning engines that meet new clean-air standards has bright prospects.

Reuters Holdings 3   RTRSY $46   0.3%
Leading worldwide electronic publisher and supplier of financial trading-room systems seeing growth in Asia and eastern Europe.

Shell Transport
& Trading   3   SC $70   3.0%
Worldwide refining and marketing business is solid

SmithKline
Beecham   3   SBE $31   3.6%
R&D efforts and marketing plans should help offset the April 1994 loss of patent protection on Tagamet anti-ulcer drug; brand names: Tums antacids, Contact cold medication, Sucret throat discs, Geritol.

Telecom Corp of
New Zealand   3   NZT $51   4.1%
Major supplier of telecommunications services is poised for growth.

Telefonos
de Mexico   5   TMX $44   2.4%
Plenty of room for telephone expansion; approval of NAFTA a big plus.

Unilever   3   UL $71   1.9%
Leading global consumer nondurable company benefiting from new acquisitions, products, and expansions; brand names: Lipton tea, Good Humor ice cream, Dove soap, Wisk laundry detergent, Pond's cream. Company is rapidly expanding into emerging markets, including China.

Waste
Management Int'l 4   WME $20   —
Has taken over almost all the operations of old company, WMX Technologies, outside North America; expansion likely to be profitable.

(Source: Standard & Poor's Corp. Top ranking: five stars. Low ranking: one star. Three to five stars indicates that S&P analysts anticipate rising revenues.)

THREE LEADING ADRs

- **Ericsson** (NASDAQ:ERICY)
  This Swedish company ranks high among the world's
  leading telecommunications firms. Its products
  include public telephone exchanges, cellular telephone
  equipment, and defense electronics. It has roughly a
  40 percent share of the worldwide market for mobile
  telephone systems and counts among its customers
  the regional Bells, McCaw Cellular Communications,
  and state-owned firms in China, Greece and Hungary.

- **Norsk Hydro** (NYSE:NYH)
  This international trading company is 51 percent
  owned by the Norwegian government. It is a leading
  crude oil and natural gas producer in the North Sea
  and also manufactures fertilizers, aluminum, magne-
  sium, and petro-chemicals. It is well positioned to capitalize on the surging Latin American and Pacific Rim
  economies, especially because of the extensive industrial base it has built in many rapidly expanding Third
  World countries.

- **Royal Dutch Petroleum** (NYSE:RD)
  This company owns 60 percent of the Royal
  Dutch/Shell Group and has a leading market share in
  50 countries with huge oil fields. It is well positioned
  to expand into Pacific Rim and Latin American countries. In a joint venture with Pemex, Mexico's national
  oil company, the Shell Oil subsidiary is upgrading a
  215,000-barrel-a-day refinery in Texas. The conver-
  sion will enable the plant to meet the standards of the
  Clean Air Act while at the same time processing large
  amounts of heavy crude oil from Pemex. The project
  is scheduled for completion in 1995. Long-term debt
  is only 10 percent of capital.

3

FOREIGN DRIPS

A number of foreign companies offer DRIPs, dividend reinvestment programs, through which you can have your dividends automatically reinvested in additional shares of the company, thus bypassing brokerage-firm costs. Many also permit direct cash purchase of shares.

Company	Industry	Telephone
Broken Hill Proprietary	Resources	(212) 648-3143
Glaxo Holdings	Drugs	(800) 524-4458
National Australia Bank	Banking	(212) 648-3143
News Corp.	Media	(212) 657-7322
Volvo AB	Autos	(212) 754-3300

4

THE MAJOR ADRS

Country	Company
Australia	**Broken Hill Properties**
	National Australia
	News Corp. Ltd.
	Pacific Dunlop
Austria	**Veitscher Magnesit**
Belgium	**Petrofina SA**
Bermuda	**ADT Ltd.**
	Jardine Matheson
Finland	**Nokla**
France	**BSN**
	Eif Aquitaine Group
	L'Oreal
	Peugeot

Germany	**BASF**
	Bayer
	Daimler-Benz
	Deutsche Bank
	Dresdner Bank
	Hoechse
	Siemens
	Thyssen
	Volkswagen
Hong Kong	**Cathay Pacific**
	China Light & Power
	Hong Kong & Shanghai Bank
	Hutchison
	Swire Pacific
Italy	**Fiat**
	Montedison
Japan	**Canon**
	Fuji Photo
	Hitachi
	Honda
	Kyocera
	Matsushita
	Mitsubishi
	Nintendo
	Nissan
	Pioneer
	Sony
	Tokio Marine & Fire
	Toyota
Malaysia	**Sime Darby**
Mexico	**Cifra**
	Group Sidek
	Ponderosa Industrial
	Telefonos de Mexico
Netherlands	**AEGON NV**
	Akzo Group
	Heineken
	Royal Dutch Petroleum
	Unilever

New Zealand	**Brierley Investments**
	Fletcher Challenge
Norway	**Hafslund Nycomed**
	Norsk Data
	Norsk Hydro
Singapore	**Development Bank**
	Keppel
	Neptune Orient Lines
South Africa	**Buffelsfontein Gold**
	DeBeers
	Kloof Gold
Spain	**Banco-Bilbao-Vizaya**
	Telefonica de Espana
Sweden	**SKF Group**
	Volvo
United Kingdom	**Barclays**
	British Airways
	British Gas
	British Petroleum
	British Steel
	British Telecom
	B.A.T. Industries
	Cable & Wireless
	Cadbury Schweppes
	Glaxo Holding
	Grand Metropolitan
	Hanson plc
	Imperial Chemical
	Manpower
	National Westminster
	Racal Telecom
	Reuters
	SmithKline Beecham

CHAPTER FOUR

U.S. MULTINATIONAL CORPORATIONS

American multinational corporations—companies with substantial portions (25 percent to 30 percent or more) of earnings and profits derived from foreign business—provide another way to invest globally and at the same time diversify your portfolio. Among the large number of large U.S. corporations that fall into this category are many household names—**Coca-Cola, IBM, Westinghouse, General Electric, Gillette, McDonald's, Exxon,** and **Mobil Oil,** to name a few. You know, for example, that almost anywhere you travel you can shave with a Gillette razor, gobble down a Big Mac, and drink a Diet Coke; that American Express has cash machines in Moscow and issues credit cards in Hungary; and that Federal Express delivers packages in Berlin, Belgrade, Belize, and Bethlehem.

ARMCHAIR INVESTING

For investors itching to get their feet wet in international markets, owning shares of a multinational company is one of the least risky choices. Albeit, multinationals are not terribly exotic, not very dramatic, yet they are an excellent way to learn about international markets without undue risk. It's not difficult to find solid, detailed research on these companies, to get copies of their annual and quarterly reports, to know what products and services they offer and how good they are.

Don't be put off by the fact that this armchair approach is an indirect route to investing abroad—if it works, it doesn't matter. If Procter & Gamble's shares rise in price because of increased foreign sales, you want to have their shares in your portfolio. And, because so many of the multinationals are also blue-chip investments, the risks are considerably lower than with individual foreign stocks.

THE CURRENT SCENE

Overseas operations of many multinationals lost some of their zip in 1993/1994 as key European economies faced recessions and Japan dealt with a myriad of problems. At the same time, U.S. export growth was sluggish. However, all things in the investment world tend to be cyclical, and so we now see that the European recession is slowly fading and multinational earnings and revenues from foreign sources are once again gathering strength. (Keep in mind, however, that despite poor corporate earnings and reduced dividends, recessions are often a smart time to buy stocks. They frequently trigger near-panic selling, providing low-priced stocks for those who can forsee a long-term recovery. Interest rates usually fall during recessions, and corporate earnings actually grow at their fastest clip as the recession moves into recovery.)

Even if in the near term some foreign markets remain soft, multinationals in the chemical, drug, household products, and computer industries are expected to generate more than a third of their sales abroad. Indeed, expansion in foreign sales and operating income has outpaced domestic growth for many of these corporations in recent years: With more than a 40 percent drop in the trade-weighted value of the dollar since 1985, they have easily boosted their share of world trade.

With new markets rapidly opening up in the European Community, the Pacific Rim, eastern Europe, South America, and elsewhere, many of the large multinationals with strong balance sheets are well positioned to take advantage of the surging demand for their products and services. In fact, the multinationals are often the first to establish a beachhold position—trade and sales agreements in the emerging market arena—as was the case with **Coca-Cola** and **Continental Grain** in China. And, as any country's economy grows and its people have more disposable income, the sales and earnings for a multinational's products and services also grow.

ADVANTAGES OF MULTINATIONAL STOCKS

Multinationals have some distinct advantages that warrant their inclusion in most portfolios. First, because they cross over a number of borders and feed into a variety of geographical markets, these companies can reap benefits when the U.S. economy slows down or moves into a recession. Second, because they are so large they can also diversify production, taking advantage of shifting economies around the globe. Third, long-term earnings growth of multinationals are frequently steadier than those of their domestic counterparts because business cycles in different areas of the world do not automatically sink and rise in unison.

Fourth, as we mentioned previously, many are blue-chip stocks.

Fifth, owning multinationals also gives you a currency play—their foreign earnings are worth more when the dollar declines and less when the dollar rises.

THE IMPORTANCE OF GOOD MANAGEMENT

Because these corporations operate within a huge, complicated global framework, management's role is critical. It must be able to direct the corporation's marketing, production, research, labor relations, and product distribution in terms of the host country's laws, regulations, and traditions. Other special factors multinationals must consider include payment of dividends in a foreign currency, owning and licensing procedures in foreign (and often unfamiliar) territories, political upheaval or risk, economic changes, and the currency factor.

Savvy Investment Tips

When selecting a multinational stock, keep in mind that: (1) when foreign currencies rise relative to the dollar, earnings from a U.S. company's foreign operations are instantly worth more; (2) a strong dollar tends to hurt the multinational stocks, as it makes U.S. products expensive for foreign buyers and foreign products cheaper for American consumers.

1

SIDE EFFECTS OF A DROP IN THE DOLLAR

- Modest rise in inflation
- Healthier U.S. stock market
- Long-term rise in interest rates
- Possible rise in gold stocks
- Rise in prices of foreign stocks

A strong dollar also creates an "exchange loss"—that is, if the money an American company earns abroad loses value against the dollar, the earnings for the company and its stockholders are reduced.

The more a U.S. multinational depends on exports for sales, the more it will benefit from a weaker dollar. Therefore, multinationals are a good hedge against a declining dollar.

And then, *select a multinational corporation that*:
1) Has a a sound management team
2) Is not overly burdened by long-term debt
3) Has products and/or services that are unique or are better than their foreign counterparts
4) Has instituted cost-cutting procedures
5) Has sizeable U.S.-generated earnings as a cushion against a decline in foreign revenues
6) Is posting rising earnings
7) Is ranked one, two, or three in timeliness and one or two in safety by *Value Line Investment Survey*

SEVEN MULTINATIONAL STOCKS TO CONSIDER

These seven stocks are well positioned to capitalize on a European, Far East and Latin American recovery and are representative of the typical, expanding multinational corporation.

- **AMP, Inc.** (NYSE:AMP)
  Based in Harrisburg, Pennsylannia, AMP is the world's leading designer and maker of electronic and electrical connectors. Its major markets are computer and office equipment, consumer goods, and transportation equipment. It is opening plants in Hungary and China and has extended its marketing reach into other areas of eastern Europe and the Near and Far East. Sales in Europe, as measured in local currencies, are growing at a modest but steady pace, and, given the recessionary climate there, this is a more than respectable showing. At the same time, the profit line is well protected by impressive sales growth in the United States.

- **Colgate-Palmolive Co.** (NYSE:CL)
  Foreign operations for this, the second largest domestic maker of detergents, toiletries, and other house-

hold products, are about 64 percent of sales. The company's Latin American and Asian/African markets are especially strong and growing rapidly; in these areas, use of personal-care products is still a novel idea, and the company's brand-name products (Palmolive, Irish Spring, Fab, Ajax, Ultra Brite, etc.) are popular. Improved manufacturing productivity, operating cost controls and ongoing growth in the developint markets should translate into continuing earnings growth for Colgate.

- **Digital Equipment** (NYSE:DEC)
  This leading manufacturer of data processing equipment has gone through an overhaul of its manufacturing and marketing operations, emerging lean and mean with improving earnings. Approximately 63 percent of its revenues are derived from abroad, 49 percent from Europe alone. A full series of computers based on its new 64-bit Alpha RISC chip will be marketed heavily through 1995. The company has a sound balance sheet, with long-term debt less than 15 percent of capitalization.

- **Nike, Inc.** (NYSE:NKE)
  This maker of athletic footwear is experiencing phenomenal demand for its shoes. Its largest growth potential, estimated to be a $12 billion market, is overseas, where revenues have been rising at more than twice the U.S. rate. In fact, more than a third of Nike's sales are made outside the United States. The company's goal is to derive 50 percent of its sales overseas by fiscal 1995, which it plans to accomplish by moving into the largely untapped markets in eastern Europe, southeast Asia, and Latin America. It is also introducing new hiking, women's, and cross-training footwear, all rapidly growing lines.

- **PepsiCo** (NYSE:PEP)
  This multinational also owns KFC (Kentucky Fried Chicken), Pizza Hut, and Taco Bell, as well as Frito-Lay, the maker of an extensive line of snack foods. The company is experiencing enormous growth in foreign markets, and as Third World citizens become more propserous, they are likely to consume vast quantities of this multinational's products.

- **Sara Lee** (NYSE:SLE)
  Formerly Consolidated Foods, this diversified international consumer packaged-goods producer focuses on coffee, specialty meats, and frozen baked goods. Foreign operations account for 35 percent of sales. Although Sara Lee is well known for its tasty cheesecake and Jimmy Dean sausage, its fastest-growing segment is its personal-products division, with Hanes hoisery and underwear and Playtex bras. Its main focus is on developing its visibility in Europe, Mexico, Asia, and central Europe. These markets are huge and fragmented, offering the company excellent growth opportunities.

- **Wrigley, (Wm), Jr.** (NYSE:WWY)
  As the world's largest manufacturer of chewing gum, the company finds it relatively easy to continue gaining market share. International gum sales are growing at double-digit rates. Its new plant in the Guang-dong province of China cannot meet demand. Shipments to eastern Europe and the former Soviet Union are rapidly increasing while Wrigley products continue to be successful in Poland and central Europe. The price of a pack of gum is Wrigley's standard 25 cents in all markets. Although this is somewhat high in regions with low costs of living, sales are expected to rise as per capita incomes increase. The company has zero debt.

A Multinational Directory

These multinationals typically obtain at least 30 percent of sales from international operations. (Source: Standard and Poor's *The Outlook*.)

Auto Industry

- Arvin Industries
- Cummins Engine
- Eaton Corp
- Echlin Inc.
- General Motors
- Goodyear Tire & Rubber
- TRW Inc.

Chemical Industry

- Cabot Corp.
- Dow Chemical
- Dupont
- Englehard Corp.
- Grace (W.R.)
- Great Lakes Chemical
- International Flavors & Fragrances
- Lubrizol Corp.
- Monsanto Co.
- Nalco Chemical
- PPG Industries
- Rohm & Haas

Computer & Software Industry

- Aldus Corp.
- Apple Computer
- Digital Equipment
- Hewlett-Packard

- International Business Machines
- Intergraph Corp.
- Microsoft Corp.
- Oracle Systems
- Seagate Technology
- Stratus Computer
- Sun Microsystems
- Tandem Computer

ELECTRONICS INDUSTRY

- AMP Inc.
- International Rectifier
- Intel Corp.
- Texas Instruments
- Varian Associates

FOOD & BEVERAGES INDUSTRY

- Coca-Cola
- CPC International
- Heinz (H.J.)
- McDonald's Corp.
- Philip Morris
- Quaker Oats
- Ralston Purina
- Sara Lee
- Wrigley, (Wm.) Jr.

HEALTH CARE INDUSTRY

- Abbott Laboratories
- American Home Products
- Bausch & Lomb
- Becton, Dickinson
- Bristol-Myers Squibb

- IMCERA Group
- Johnson & Johnson
- Merck & Co.
- Pfizer Inc.
- Schering-Plough
- Warner Lambert

HOUSEHOLD PRODUCTS INDUSTRY

- Avon Products
- Black & Decker
- Gillette Co.
- Halliburton Co.
- Nike, Inc.
- Premark International
- Procter & Gamble
- Reebok International

MACHINERY & ENGINEERING INDUSTRIES

- Beckman Instruments
- Crown Cork & Seal
- Foster Wheeler
- Harnischfeger Industries
- Ingersoll-Rand
- Keystone International
- TRINOVA Corp.

OTHER

- Eastman Kodak
- Emerson Electric
- Honeywell Inc.
- ITT Corp.
- Millipore Corp.
- Minnesota Mining & Manufacturing (MMM)

- Perkin-Elmer
- Polaroid Corp.
- United Technologies
- Xerox Corp.

CHAPTER FIVE

BRADY BONDS: HIGH-YIELDING FOREIGN DOLLAR INVESTMENTS

If you are looking for high yields but do not judge the current returns on junk bonds to be worth their risk, one new alternative is funds that invest in "Brady bonds"—the U.S. dollar debt of developing countries, particularly Latin America. Double-digit returns are attracting investors to such funds; and though their high yields go hand-in-hand with greater risk, Brady bonds have an advantage that Donald Trump's bonds do not—the U.S. government assures that they will be repaid.

THE SEARCH FOR HIGHER YIELDS

The natural reaction to low interest rates is to look elsewhere for a higher return, yet there is a point past which investors should not chase after yield at the expense of an investment's safety. How bad did it get? During his 1993 confirmation hearings, Arthur Leavitt Jr., chairman of the U.S. Securities and Exchange Commission, disclosed that he owns $50,000 to $100,000 of Bulgarian currency, most likely in the form of Bulgarian government Treasury bills. Is that what the normal investor should do—open the monthly statement, gasp at how little the money fund is paying, then rush out and buy Bulgarian T-bills? Although some nimble professional probably knows what affects such faraway local currency debt markets (and can get out at a moment's notice), most investors are advised to more prudently weigh safety against the prospect of increased yield. Before considering a high-risk/high-yield bond in a foreign currency, take a look at the advantages of Brady bonds, which are high-yielding foreign investments *denominated in U.S. dollars*.

HOW BRADY BONDS BEGAN

Not long ago, Latin American economies were staggering under massive foreign debts. In 1982, Mexico threatened to default on its international bank loans, many of which had been made by large U.S. banks. Latin America became the last place banks wanted to lend money, yet countries there were desperate to reinvigorate their economies, and that slim prospect was the only hope that lenders had of getting paid back.

To resolve the situation, then–Treasury Secretary Nicholas Brady proposed a plan to turn the U.S. commercial bank loans into bonds. The idea was for the banks to give Latin American countries a break, either by lowering the rate of interest on their U.S. loans or by forgiving some of their debt. In effect, the banks agreed to take back the loans they had made to Latin American countries and, in return, received Brady bonds that they could easily sell because the bonds were guaranteed to be paid off, something that had been highly unlikely with the old loans. The South American debtor countries also pledged to implement market reforms, but the U.S. banks greeted that promise with skepticism.

MEXICO'S SUCCESS ENCOURAGES OTHER BRADY BOND DEALS

In 1990, Mexico became the first country to restructure its debt under the Brady plan when it swapped $43.5 billion of debt for $36.2 billion of Brady bonds. And Mexico did follow through with market reforms. It lowered its inflation, cut back on government spending, and stabilized its currency. The price of Mexican Brady bonds soared.

The success of Mexico's Brady bonds had two impacts:

- It encouraged other countries to complete similar debt restructurings. By early 1994, after Brazil completed its $40 billion debt restructuring, more than $120 billion of Brady bonds were outstanding.

- Investors became bullish on Brady bonds. Through 1993, over $10 billion poured into Latin American bond markets, three times the previous year's total.

BRADY BOND ADVANTAGES

A FOREIGN INVESTMENT WITH NO CURRENCY RISK

Brady bonds are U.S.-dollar bonds issued by developing countries that have restructured their outstanding debt under terms of the so-called "Brady Plan," named for its creator, U.S. Treasury Secretary Nicholas Brady. Interest and principal payments are made in U.S. dollars.

SAFETY: THEY ARE BACKED BY U.S. GOVERNMENT BONDS

Each issuing country is responsible for making periodic interest payments on its Brady bonds, but most of the bonds are backed by U.S. government Treasury securities—zero coupon bonds that pay out one lump sum at maturity. These U.S. Treasury securities are legally a part of the Brady bonds and effectively guarantee their repayment at maturity. They work like this:

- When a Brady bond comes due, the same amount of U.S. government zero coupon bonds will mature in one balloon payment.

- Then the proceeds from the "zeros" are paid directly to the holders of the Brady bonds.

This effective U.S. government guarantee of the principal has a profound impact on the relative risk of Brady bonds compared with junk bonds. If a junk bond defaults, an investor can lose his or her entire investment. But if a Brady bond defaults, the most an investor can lose is the remaining interest payments due on the bond; thanks to the U.S. Treasury securities that back Brady bonds, the investor will receive the face amount of the bond when it reaches maturity.

HISTORICALLY HIGHER YIELDS

The 1993 yields on the most widely traded Latin American bonds ranged from 8.5 percent to 14 percent. The total returns were even higher because of the appreciation of the bonds themselves. According to the J.P. Morgan Emerging Markets Bond Index, Brady bonds issued by developing countries generated a total return to investors of nearly 30 percent in 1993. By contrast, the returns of 79 U.S. corporate high-yield (junk bond) funds tracked by Morningstar averaged 13.8 percent.[1]

UNDERSTANDING THE RISKS

For investors considering Brady bonds, the Latin American debt crash of 1982 is grounds for caution. Economic reforms in many Brady bond countries are spurring on progress, but more time is needed before these reforms take root in the political and social traditions. Investors should also consider these additional risks:

---

1. The average SEC yield of 79 high-yield corporate bond funds tracked by Morningstar as of September 6, 1994.

- The bond issuers are sovereign countries. If a country does not meet its interest payments, there is little redress an investor can expect to find from U.S. courts.

- From their inception in 1990 through 1993 Brady bonds had a spectacular bull run. It is worth noting that no country has defaulted on paying interest on its Brady bonds, but if one did, the whole market could abruptly drop in price.

- If U.S. interest rates rise dramatically, Brady bonds will decline in value. Interest rates on some Brady bonds are adjusted up or down according to changing market conditions, but many pay fixed rates of interest. U.S. interest rates, in general, have declined markedly over the past decade, and this has benefited fixed-rate investments. However, should this trend reverse and cause U.S. Treasury bonds to decline in price, the value of Brady bonds would likely follow.

Funds That Invest in Restructured Debt

Several funds invest in the debt of developing countries. Before these funds were launched, only institutional investors or very wealthy individuals had access to the market. This market remains complex, making it imperative that most individuals invest in these bonds through a specialized fund, which offers diversification, professional management and portfolio supervision. As with any category of mutual fund, compare track records and fees. Also check what debt instruments a fund is allowed to invest in. Some funds allow holdings of pre-Brady restructured debt, as was the case for Brazil's dollar debt in 1993, or even nonperforming loans, both of which are riskier than Brady bond debt. The fund management team should have ten or more years of investing experience in interest-rate markets because Brady bonds will be affected by general shifts, higher or lower, in interest rates.

CLOSED-END FUNDS   SEPT. 1994 YIELD

Alliance World Dollar
Government (AWG)   12.3%
Alliance Capital Management runs this top-performing fund. It invests at least 75% of fund assets in Brady bonds, throughout the world, and U.S. zero coupon bonds. Phone: (800) 247-4154.

Latin America
Dollar Income (LBF)   10.6%
Scudder, Stevens & Clark restricts its focus to Latin America, where most Brady bonds are located. Phone: (617) 330-5602

MUTUAL FUNDS   CURRENT YIELD

G.T. Global High Income 7.2%
G.T. Global Financial Services runs this open-end mutual fund which was the first to focus on the debt securities of developing economies around the world. Phone: (800) 824-1580.

Fidelity New
Markets Income   9.19%

This new fund got off to a fast start, turning in a sizzling 11.63% for its first full quarter to September 1993. It invests primarily in Latin debt. Phone: (800) 544-8888.

III

INVESTING WITH THE PACK: USING FOREIGN MUTUAL FUNDS

CHAPTER SIX

A MUTUAL FUND PRIMER

Despite all the compelling reasons for investing abroad, doing so remains risky, riskier than staying at home: There are fewer regulations protecting investors, a relative lack of reliable information, complicated tax situations, different settlement practices. Add to this what Wall Streeters like to call "event" risk: revolutions, earthquakes, revolutions, even governmental seizure of a company's assets. Such happenings could, indeed, wipe out investment gains.

That's why mutual funds, which are professionally managed, are a sensible solution for those who don't want to fly solo through foreign lands. If you don't have the time, inclination, skill, or sufficient capital to select your own stocks and bonds, you've plenty of mutual-fund alternatives. You're undoubtedly already well acquainted with funds—one in four American households invests in them. If you are, you can skip the section explaining their advantages and disadvantages, but before you do, make certain that you *really* understand the critical differences between the two types of funds: open-end and closed-end.

A Mutual Fund Primer: Understanding the Basics

Mutual funds are investment companies that pool money from thousands of individuals. As the investment company takes in this money, it issues shares directly to buyers and then invests the money in a diversified portfolio. Each share in a fund represents ownership of part of the fund's portfolio of underlying securities. Depending upon the goals of the fund, the portfolio may consist of stocks, bonds, foreign currencies, cash, and money market instruments. Funds range in purpose and philosophy from conservative to daring, from owning money market instruments to junk bonds.

The term "open-end" means that the fund doesn't have a set number of shares but issues new shares as it takes in money from investors and redeems shares as investors withdraw or sell their shares back to the fund. This easy ability to move in and out of funds, known as liquidity, is one of their greatest strengths.

Closed-end funds, often called "country funds," have a set number of shares and trade on the stock exchanges or over the counter. They invest in diversified portfolios of stocks and bonds and are discussed in Chapter 9.

Benefits

The key advantages of mutual funds are:

- *Diversification.* Funds have sufficient capital to buy a great many individual stocks and bonds, far more, obviously, than any individual can afford. Such wide diversification reduces the risk factor of investing. Because each share represents proportionate ownership, an investors who purchases $1,000 worth of shares has the same percentage of profits and losses as someone who owns $10,000 worth of shares.

- *Professional management.* Experts buy, sell, or hold securities based on continually updated economic data.
- *Services.* With many of the larger mutual-fund companies you can also purchase individual stocks and bonds through the fund's discount brokerage arm (if it has one), write checks against certain types of funds, handle many transactions by telephone, and take advantage of automatic investment programs.

DETERMINING PRICE AND VALUE

A fund's price is based on its net asset value (NAV) per share—that is, the value of all the investments the fund owns minus its liabilities, divided by the number of existing shares. If that value increases, so does the share price, and vice versa.

Unlike stocks, whose prices typically change with each trade, mutual-fund NAVs are calculated only once a day—at the close of trading. At that time, the fund is required by law to total the value of the securities in its portfolio.

BUYING FUNDS

Open-end mutual funds are purchased either through stockbrokers (such as the Alliance Capital, Putnam, and Franklin funds), through banks, or directly from a sponsoring investment company (such as T. Rowe Price, Fidelity, Twentieth Century, Vanguard, Scudder, or Harbor). The third group, funds that are sold directly to the public through toll-free telephone numbers, the mail or, in some cities, walk-in offices, are called "no-load" funds because they do not charge a sales fee. Even no-load funds, however, may have some fees: redemption fees when you sell shares, a marketing charge called a 12b-1 fee that covers the fund's marketing and advertising costs, or other transaction fees.

Funds sold by brokerage firms charge a sales load, which can range from under 3 percent to a maximum of 8.5 percent and therefore are called "load funds." Some brokerage firms, such as Merrill Lynch and PaineWebber, sell only their own, in-house funds. Should you buy funds that charge a sales fee? If you can't decide which fund to invest in and your broker can, then the answer is yes. And, in some cases, load funds turn in such juicy returns that it's worth the fee to participate. However, as Sheldon Jacobs, publisher of *The Handbook for No-Load Investors* explains, there's no firm evidence that paying a load automatically gets you a superior return. If you study no-load fund returns carefully, you, too, can pick winners.

TRACKING PERFORMANCE AND PRICE

You can track a fund's performance by following several figures: first, its share price or Net Asset Value (NAV); second, its yield—the amount of income it produces; third, its total return—income plus any capital gains or losses after expenses. Although all three are important, only the total return figure gives a complete judgment because it combines profits from dividends, profits from gains in the portfolio, and the fund's costs. When comparing one fund with another, the total return figure is the best measure. Bear in mind, too, that in a growth stock fund, yield or dividends are not as important as price appreciation, whereas in a bond fund, yield is critical. Obviously you can't turn your back on a bond fund's share prices either. *Barron's* publishes a comprehensive survey of mutual fund performance figures every quarter. This pull-out section, called "Barron's/Lipper Mutual Fund Quarterly," gives three-month, one-year, and five-year performance figures, sales load, dividend yield, the amount of money under management, the name of the portfolio manager and how long he or she has been there, and the toll-free telephone number.

Money magazine and *Kiplinger's Personal Finance* magazine give similar information on a monthly basis. *Forbes, Business Week, U.S. News & World Report,* and *Your Money* cover funds less frequently, but each publication puts its own interesting spin on the facts. For a more in-depth, analytical analysis of individual funds, check issues of *Morningstar* and *Value Line* (see Appendix for details).

THE PROSPECTUS

Although there's plenty of research waiting to be read, in order to fully understand a fund's investment purpose, its costs, and risk level, you should also read its prospectus, a document that the SEC requires the fund to give to prospective investors. It's true, of course, that only serious number-crunching types actually want to read it. Yet the prospectus does spell out the fund's costs, fees, objectives, and what types of investments it may purchase. You'll also find out, in addition to stocks and bonds, for instance, if a fund can hold options, warrants, or currency future contracts and if it participates in hedging. Nevertheless, one important piece of information, a list of the fund's holdings, is seldom found in the prospectus; you must ask for the separate "Statement of Additional Information" (SAI), and, for the most recent listing, the fund's latest quarterly report.

TYPES OF FOREIGN FUNDS

When researching mutual funds that invest abroad you will encounter several types; each is further described in Part 4.

- *Global bond*: Buys corporate and government bonds from all parts of the globe, including the United States.
- *Global equity*: Buys stocks from all parts of the globe, including the United States.

- *International equity*: Buys at least two-thirds of its holdings outside the United States.
- *Precious metals and gold*: Buys stocks of companies that mine gold and other metals.
- *Closed-end country funds*: Buys stocks or bonds, often of just one country or area; shares trade on the exchanges or over the counter.

INVESTMENT TIPS

When picking a fund, keep these eight points in mind:

1) If you're taking your first step onto the international playing field, begin with a diversified fund as opposed to a country or regional fund. It is less susceptible to risk.
2) The more diversified you are, the less likely you'll be hit by poor results from any one stock or market.
3) Unless you're a sophisticated investor, stay clear of funds too new to have a track record.
4) Compare the total return figures for one and five years.
5) When studying these return figures, pay careful attention to whether sales charges and other fees are taken into account.
6) The obvious advantage of a no-load fund is that all your money is invested; however, excellent management by a load fund may offset that. Again, compare total return figures for several funds within the same category.
7) Don't put all your eggs in one mutual-fund basket or family; diversify to gain the benefits of different management styles, expertise, and economic viewpoints.
8) If you're putting money into an equity fund, check the record date for distributions. If you purchase shares just before a large capital gains distribution, you may incur a tax liability. Wait until after the distribution to buy: The fund's NAV will be lower by the amount of distribution, and you won't wind up paying taxes on holdings the fund sold at a profit before you bought shares.

CHAPTER SEVEN

INVESTING FOR HIGH INCOME: FOREIGN BOND FUNDS

Anyone looking for a nice steady stream of fixed income dislikes low interest rates—yet that's precisely what Americans have been faced with in recent years, with yields on savings accounts, certificates of deposit, Treasury issues, and even corporate bonds at all-time lows. Investing in fixed-income securities with a foreign flavor can be one way to circumvent this situation.

Although economic conditions vary widely around the globe, at any one point there are countries where interest rates on government and corporate bonds are higher than in the United States. In addition to high yields, these foreign bonds also provide a way to profit from declines in the U.S. dollar and at the same time reduce the risk of holding an all-U.S. portfolio: Foreign and domestic markets move independently, so any losses in one can be offset by gains in the other. You may wonder why many foreign bonds pay higher rates than their U.S. counterparts. Interest rates generally reflect both a country's economic situation and its government's monetary policies. Often many foreign governments make greater efforts to control inflation than the United States and their tight monetary policies keep interest rates high. When the dollar is weak, as it was in 1985, 1986, 1987, 1990 and 1992, foreign bonds have better returns than domestic ones, based on interest payments, price appreciation, and the currency situation. We refer to this as the three C's—coupon, capital and currency. When the dollar is strong, however, foreign bond funds underperform U.S. issues.

There are plenty of opportunities to capture these potentially higher foreign yields: More than half of all fixed-income securities are traded abroad. The vast majority are traded electronically in over-the-counter markets, and information on them is available to international traders and portfolio managers by high-speed computers and satelite communications. In fact, many bonds trade around the clock. You can participate either through mutual funds or by purchasing individual bonds.

In this chapter we will look at short-term global income funds and longer-term global and international funds. "Global" funds invest worldwide, including in the United States, and therefore have significantly less currency risk than "international" funds that exclude U.S. investments except, perhaps, for their reserves (typically 10 percent of net assets). "World" funds may or may not invest in the United States.

If you are unfamiliar with how the bond market works, take time to read the next section, "A Bond Primer: Understanding the Basics." Otherwise, skip ahead to "Currency Risks."

A BOND PRIMER: UNDERSTANDING THE BASICS

A bond is really like an IOU. It is an official interest-bearing security issued by a government, a governmental agency, municipality, or a corporation to raise money. The investor or bondholder is actually lending money to the issuer for a stated period of time. The amount lent, called the principal, is paid back in full at a specified maturity date. This date can be anywhere from several months to many years. During this time, the issuer (i.e., the borrower) agrees to pay the lender interest for the use of the money. This interest rate, called the coupon rate, is fixed—it does not change during the life of the bond. If, for example, an investor who purchases a bond for $1,000 with a coupon rate of 7 percent will receive $35 every six months until the bond matures. Upon maturity the principal ($1,000) will be returned.

Bonds can be issued for almost any number of years, although the maximum is generally thirty. Those with maturity dates under ten years are called notes.

Although a bond's interest rate remains the same throughout its life, its price does not. When a bond is first issued it is sold at face value, usually $1,000. After that it trades in the secondary market, on an exchange or over the counter, and its price continually fluctuates along with changes in interest rates. The first rule of thumb to keep in mind is:

BOND PRICES MOVE IN THE OPPOSITE DIRECTION OF INTEREST RATES

If interest rates rise, the value of a bond will decline, and vice versa. For example, if a bond is purchased at face value ($1,000) with a coupon or interest rate of 8 percent, the bondholder will receive $80 in interest payments annually. If interest rates move up and the same corporation issues new bonds to raise money, it is forced to pay a higher rate, say 9 percent or $90 a year. The corporation's older bonds will then fall in price, with the newly issued ones being more prized for their higher yield.

This relationship between interest rates and bond prices is often overlooked or misunderstood by investors, especially those accustomed to having money in bank certificates of deposit, where the value does not change. The same is true with money market funds, which are priced at $1 per share, so your account has as many shares as it has dollars. This is not the case with bonds or bond mutual funds. Even if a bond fund is made up of U.S. Treasuries or insured municipal bonds, its value can shoot up or down.

The second rule of thumb:

The Longer the Bond's Maturity, the More Sensitive It Is to Interest-rate Changes

The creditworthiness of the issuer can be evaluated if its bonds are rated. Two major independent services, Moody's Investor Services and Standard & Poor's, list their ratings in continually revised books that are available at libraries and brokerage firms.

Ratings range from AAA (the best quality) to D (in default). Investment-grade bonds are rated AAA, AA, A, or BBB by Standard & Poor's, or Aaa, Aa, A, or Baa by Moody's. A bond below investment grade is known as high-yield debt, or a "junk" bond. Within the junk category, bonds rated BB and B are sometimes referred to as "quality junk" and may be bonds of formerly blue-chip companies that have assumed huge amounts of debt in leveraged buyouts, takeovers, or some other form of financial restructuring.

Individual Bonds versus Mutual Funds

Mutual funds have many well-touted advantages, chief among them diversification, yet within the international bond fund category their biggest plus is professional management. These experts have immediate access to information on foreign economies and governments, to first-hand research, to the ever-changing currency situation. They live and breathe the international scene. They are also able to trade their fund's assets on a daily basis, aiming for high returns while at the same time hedging against unfavorable interest-rate movement and currency exchange rates—things individual investors are ill equipped to do.

However, even the best fund managers can't protect their portfolios on all sides, especially when interest rates drop. When this happens and new money comes into the fund, they cannot invest it at as high a rate as had been possible previously. The new money buys bonds with lower yields, and thus the earnings of the fund eventually start to fall. The fund's monthly income payout also drops—although not immediately. And, if interest rates climb, there isn't too much the manager can do to prevent the fund's asset value from falling. (Net asset value [NAV] per share, also known as the fund's per share price, is determined at the end of the trading day, at 4:00 P.M. eastern time each day the New York Stock Exchange is open. Each fund's share price is calculated by subtracting its liabilities from its total assets and dividing the result by the total number of shares outstanding. Liabilities include accrued expenses and dividends payable; total assets include portfolio securities valued at market plus income accrued but not yet received.) The NAV is listed in the financial pages of most newspapers.

Having examined the pros and cons of funds, let's look at the pluses and minuses for owning individual bonds. First of all, when you own a specific bond, you know what your annual income will be and the dollar amount you will receive if you hold the bonds to maturity. And with individual bonds, you know how long it is until that maturity date when your principal is paid back. If you have, say, a twelve-year bond, you know that next year it will be an eleven-year bond, a ten-year bond the following year, and so on. In twelve years it will mature. A bond fund, on the other hand, never matures. If the fund's mission is to keep the portfolio around four years or ten years or some other number, it will keep trading the bonds in the portfolio to meet this aim. With a fund your investment (what you initially paid for the shares) will be retrieved if, when you go to sell, the shares are worth the same as or more than you paid for them.

CURRENCY RISKS AND HEDGING

Before fleeing low-yielding domestic investments, however, consider the downside—currency risk. All foreign bond funds face currency risks, regardless of the quality or maturity of the bonds in the fund's portfolio. That's because the dollar must be converted to the local currency to purchase foreign bonds. Then, any interest earned and any sale or redemption proceeds must be converted again, from the foreign currency back into U.S. dollars. Because foreign exchange rates change continually, the bond's dollar value can increase or decrease, even if its price remains unchanged. Specifically, a rising dollar can spell disaster for investors in foreign bonds because when the dollar rises in value against foreign currencies, bonds (or stocks) denominated in those currencies are worth fewer dollars. A decline in the dollar, however, can produce extra gains.

Currency risk, in fact, is a more critical factor to consider when investing in foreign bonds than is current yield. For example, during the first quarter of 1993, the yen rose against the dollar, and the total return of Japanese bonds in the Salomon Brothers World Government Bond Index was only 1.84 percent in local currency but 14.51 percent in dollars. By contrast, a 5.9 percent return from Swedish bonds in krona became 2.5 percent in dollars during the same period. Because of such fluctuations, foreign bond funds should be viewed as long-term investments so as to ride out currency fluctuations.

HEDGING

Many foreign fixed-income funds reduce foreign exchange rate exposure through a technique called hedging. There are several types of hedges. In a *direct hedge*, a U.S. investor buying a one-year French bond, for example, buys a contract to sell French francs for dollars a year later at a price agreed upon when the contract is purchased. In this way, the investor eliminates currency price risk as an unknown factor. Fund managers will use a direct hedge back into the U.S. dollar if they want to eliminate nearly all of the risk of owning a particular currency or if they think the portfolio will benefit from price appreciation in a given country's bonds but do not want to hold the currency.

But a direct hedge has several drawbacks: It eliminates the possibility of gain from currency fluctuations—that's what you give up to prevent a loss—and the forward contract is priced to equal the difference between the yields on the U.S. and French short-term securities. If this difference at the time is wide because U.S. rates are far lower than French rates, the hedge will be expensive and thus will reduce the investor's total return on the French bond.

Another type of hedge, the *cross hedge*, is used to reduce the disadvantages found in the direct hedge. The investor or portfolio manager buys a bond with a strong currency and goes short or sells a weaker currency. Or, to state it another way, if a particular currency is expected to decrease against another, a fund manager may sell the currency expected to decrease and purchase a bond in a currency that is expected to increase against the currency sold. He will sell in an amount about the same as the fund's holdings denominated in the currency sold. The degree to which cross hedging is successful depends largely on currencies remaining within a certain range relative to each other. Although cross hedging is less expensive than a direct hedge, it still cuts the overall return on the foreign bond. And it's not risk-free: It assumes that currencies will remain within a certain range or band.

Hedging techniques can also include use of swaps and options, which are more complicated but may be cheaper, although most managers hedge weaker currencies against stronger ones. Hedging can cost 2.5 percent to 5 percent of the value of the assets being hedged. Costs are treated as capital transactions and are not reflected in a fund's yield but rather in its Net Asset Value. (That's another reason why a fund's yield should not be taken as a completely accurate indicator of total return.)

Currency risk is not the only headache; foreign bonds are accompanied by a rash of potential problems: that the bonds may be called early, that the issuer may default (unless it's a government bond), that some of the bonds may be illiquid, that accurate information about a given foreign market may be difficult to come by—all factors pointing to using mutual funds as a way to play this segment of the global market.

PICKING A FOREIGN BOND FUND

Although foreign bond funds often use the word *income* in their names, this does not mean that your income is guaranteed or that the fund's per share price will not drop. These funds are not a substitute for domestic bonds or bond funds. Indeed, these funds can be extremely volatile, with returns rising sharply one year, declining the next. And, as we keep emphasizing, if the value of the dollar rises against foreign currencies, you could get whipsawed. Their stormy history does not mean they should be shunned, however. They can provide hefty yields and wide diversification.

UNDERSTANDING A FUND'S TOTAL RETURN

When doing research on foreign bond funds you'll need to know and compare a fund's total return figure for the year to date and the past one and five years. Total return or the measure of a fund's performance includes yield (dividend, interest, and capital gains) as well as changes in the per share price, or NAV, of the fund over a designated time. This figure is given in the fund's prospectus and many financial publications, such as *Money*, *Your Money*, and others. Funds that are sold directly to investors give out this figure to those who call the fund's toll-free number.

The total return figure for foreign bond funds is based on the three C's: coupon (the interest income), capital (the price gain or loss for the bonds in the portfolio), and currency (gain or loss of one currency against another). The total return is equal to the sum of these three components.

Funds may advertise total return figures on both a cumulative and compound average annual basis and then compare them with indices, such as the S&P 500, and with other mutual funds. Cumulative total return compares the amount invested at the beginning of a given time period with the amount redeemed at the end of the period, assuming that all dividends and capital gains are reinvested. The compound average annual total return shows a yearly compound average of a fund's performance, derived from the cumulative total return. A fund may advertise a yield figure based on dividing the fund's net investment income per share during a thirty-day base period by the per share price on the last day of the base period.

The total return figure and the yield are defined by SEC regulations. Here are the factors to consider:

1) *Interest income.* This is quite simply the interest paid by the foreign bonds. The interest payments are made in the currency in which the bond is denominated. So, for example, a Swiss government bond makes periodic interest payments in Swiss francs. In a mutual fund, the interest received is then converted into U.S. dollars and paid out, net of the fund's expenses, in the form of dividends. Investors may take the dividends in cash or elect to have them reinvested in additional fund shares. Foreign bonds may or may not pay higher interest rates than U.S. bonds.

2) *Bond price gain or loss.* Bond prices always move in the opposite direction of interest rates. In a declining Swiss interest-rate environment, for example, the prices on

existing Swiss bonds will rise. When Swiss interest rates rise, the opposite is true—the bonds will decline in price. The degree of bond price movement is directly proportional to the maturity of the bond, so the bonds with the longest maturities will have the greatest gains or losses when interest rates move.

3) *Currency gain or loss.* The price of a foreign currency denominated bond, when translated into U.S. dollars, will move up and down with changes in the exchange rate between the foreign currency and the dollar. For example, any increase in the value of the Swiss franc versus the U.S. dollar will cause the dollar value of Swiss bonds to increase. Conversely, any rise in the dollar reduces the dollar value of Swiss bonds.

Because the bond price and the currency exchange rate can each be positive or negative over time, the total return for a fund may be higher or lower than the yield alone. If a fund has a 10 percent yield but only a 3 percent total return, it lost 7 percent of its Net Asset Value during the time period being measured. This concept is illustrated in the accompanying box.

4) *Other Factors to Consider*

•Foreign bond funds typically are more volatile than their domestic counterparts because of currency fluctuations.

•Foreign bond portfolio strategies vary widely from conservative funds, such as **MFS Worldwide Government** and **Scudder International Bond**, which restrict holdings of below-investment-grade debt (rated below BBB) to 10 percent to 15 percent of assets.

•More aggressive funds, such as **Fidelity Global Bond** and **GT Global Strategic Income** focus more on emerging country debt, including Brady bonds.

•Because these funds require expertise and continual monitoring, their expense ratios range from 1.20 percent to 1.85 percent compared with about 1 percent for domestic bond funds.

SEVEN GUIDELINES

Follow these seven investment guidelines when selecting a foreign bond fund:

1) *Know* whether you want a short-term or longer-term fund, or both. The shorter the term of the bonds in the portfolio, the lower the risk. Throughout the first half of 1994, the total return of the eighty-six general world income funds, those that invest in dollar and nondollar denominated debt of assorted maturities, tracked by Lipper Analytical Services, was down about three percentage points below U.S. government funds.

2) *Keep* shares for several years to even out their price volatility.

3) *Reduce* your risk factor by looking to funds that also hold bonds in the U.S. dollar bloc: Canada, Mexico, Australia, and New Zealand. It may mean a lower yield, but it also means lower currency risk.

4) *Find out* the Moody and S&P ratings for the bonds in the portfolio as well as what percentage are nonrated or rated below A. Are there too many junk bonds for your comfort level? The higher the creditworthiness of the issuer, the lower your risk, and usually the lower the yield.

5) *Read* a professional evaluation of the fund. Hedging practices vary considerably, making fund evaluation difficult. We believe that the only way to fully evaluate a fund is by studying its track record, using information published by *Lipper Analytic, Value Line,* and *Morningstar* (see Appendix).

6) *Compare* the annual total return figures for several funds. (see below).

7) *Invest* cautiously in funds too new to have a track record.

SHORT-TERM GLOBAL INCOME FUNDS

Among the foreign bond funds, short-term global funds have the greatest share price stability. They also tend to have higher yields than money market funds, and although their Net Asset Values are stable, they are not as stable as those of money market funds.

As their name implies, they invest in high-quality foreign and U.S. fixed-income securities that typically mature in three years or fewer. These securities include government debt, short-term commercial paper and CDs, debentures, mortgage-based securities, and money market instruments issued throughout the world. Some hold a portion of their assets in dollar-denominated and foreign securities. For example, **Fidelity's Short-Term World Income Fund**, yielding nearly 7 percent in early 1994, is primarily invested in the United States, Canada, Sweden, France, Mexico, and Italy. It aims to purchase A-rated securities, yet up to 35 percent of its assets may be in BBB- or BB- rated securities and within that 35 percent, only 10 percent in BB debt.

The fact that maturities are short helps reduce the effect of interest-rate fluctuations. The values of the bonds do not rise as much when foreign interest rates fall, nor do values fall as much when foreign interest rates rise (see box). Although these funds are often marketed as relatively low-risk alternatives to money market funds or certificates of deposit, don't be misled. They are not a substitue for either. First of all, their share price, unlike that of a money market fund, will fluctuate with interest rate *and* currency swings. In fact, the currency risk factor makes them suitable only for those willing to accept share price volatility. To illustrate this point: In September 1992, several European countries unhappy with the Bundesbank's high lending rates, devalued their own currencies. As a result, the NAVs of the short-term global income funds fell. (Domestic money market funds, on the other hand, hold their per share prices at $1.00.) Nor are all holdings in a short-term fund necessarily triple A-rated. Finally, the principal in these funds is not insured or guaranteed, as is the case with bank CDs and Treasury issues. Many short-term global bond funds also have high expense ratios, averaging about 1.5 percent or more, which is nearly three times that of domestic money market funds.

Among the oldest of these short-term global funds is the **Alliance Short-Term Multi-Market Trust**, started in 1989. The fund's shares have been impressively stable—$9.70 when first sold and around $10 as of late 1994.

The fund invests in securities that mature in fewer than three years—government debt, CDs, corporate short-term paper, all rated AA by Standard & Poor's. The fund keeps at least 25 percent in U.S. dollar denominated paper, which reduces its currency risk but also its potential return. With some 75 percent in foreign debt, it has a large exposure to currency risk, and so the fund manager uses cross hedging—buying a long, high-yielding currency and selling short a lower yielding currency. (Selling short means selling a security you do not own but have borrowed from a stockbroker, in anticipation that you will be able to buy it later at a lower price. In other words, you are betting that the price will drop.)

An interesting newcomer, the **North American Government Income Fund**, run by the Trust Company of the West for Dean Witter, invests up to 25 percent of its assets in Mexican Treasury bills (Cetes), up to 10 percent in Canadian government bills, and the balance in U.S. government–guaranteed securities. The fund's yield has been around 7 percent.

1

FIVE SHORT-TERM GLOBAL INCOME FUNDS

Fund/Telephone	Sales Fee	Sept. 1994 Yield
Alliance Short-Term Multi-Market Class A (800) 221-5672	4 1/4%	7.3%
Blanchard Short-Term Global Income (800) 922-7771	none	7.5%
Eaton Vance Short-Term Global (800) 225-6265	3%	7.5%
Fidelity Short-Term World Income (800) 544-8888	none	7.4%
Scudder Short-Term Global Income (800) 225-2470	none	7.3%

FOREIGN BOND FUNDS

Income and appreciation are the hallmarks of funds that invest in longer-term foreign bonds. Most of these funds are not just foreign funds but are "global" funds because they include some U.S. bonds in their portfolios. Their average bond maturity is six years.

The individual funds in this group have differing requirements governing what securities they can invest in. These details and the bond ratings, when available, are spelled out in the fund's prospectus. Some, such as the **T. Rowe Price Global Government Bond Fund**, invest primarily in high-quality U.S. and foreign government bonds. The **Kidder Peabody Global Fixed Income Fund** is almost 100 percent invested in government issues with AAA or equivalent credit ratings, with an average maturity of a little under six years. The fund has bonds in three separately managed geographical areas: Europe, the Pacific Basin, and North America. The **T. Rowe Price International Bond Fund** invests in nondollar denominated high-quality government and corporate bonds rated A or better. A more aggressive (translation: risky) philosophy allows the **GT Global High Income Fund** to buy debt of emerging countries such as Mexico and Argentina.

The three foreign bond funds listed among the forty-six best funds by Warren Boronson in his book *The Ultimate Mutual Fund Guide: 17 Experts Pick the 46 Top Funds You Should Own* are **Scudder International Bond**, **T. Rowe Price International Bond**, and **Fidelity Global Bond**.

2

TOTAL RETURN FOR FOREIGN BONDS

When bond prices move	When currency rates move	The total return vs. the bond's yield is
higher	higher	uncertain
higher	equal	lower
uncertain	lower	lower

3

SIX INTERNATIONAL BOND FUNDS

Fund/Telephone	Sales Fee	Current Yield as of Sept. 1994
GT Global Government Income A (800) 824-1580	4.75%	6.68%
GT Global Strategic Income A (800) 824-1580	4.75%	6.8%
Fidelity Global Bond (800) 544-8888	none	8.03%
T. Rowe Price International Bond (800) 638-5660	none	5.83%
Scudder International Bond (800) 225-2470	none	8.43%
Merrill Lynch World Income A (800) 637-3863	4.00%	8.25%

4

HOW INTEREST-RATE CHANGES IMPACT BOND PRICES

Movements in rates have more effect on prices of longer-term bonds than on those with shorter maturities. The following table, courtesy of T. Rowe Price, shows the effect of a one percentage point change in interest rates on a $1,000 bond with a 7 percent coupon.

Bond—Maturity	Principal value if rates:	
	Increase by 1%:	Decrease by 1%:
2 years	$982	$1,019
5 years	$959	$1,043
20 years	$901	$1,116

INDIVIDUAL FOREIGN BONDS

Sophisticated investors can buy foreign bonds directly through some U.S. stockbrokers. The World Bank, for example, has been a leading issuer of global bonds since it launched the first one in 1989. Citibank, a unit of Citicorp, also markets issues. If your broker does not handle foreign bonds, and many do not, he or she can direct you to a firm that does, but be prepared for high minimum requirements—anywhere from $25,000 to $100,000. Building a portfolio of individual bonds is best left to high-income people who plan to hold the bonds to maturity. A key advantage in holding bonds until maturity is that at that date you receive the full face value, whereas when you sell shares in a mutual fund they may be worth more or less than you paid originally—funds must mark the value of their portfolios at the end of each day, and this is reflected in the fund's per share price. The price will vary from day to day, based on the direction of interest rates and the swing in currencies.

If you buy bonds directly and stick to medium- to long-term bonds, you can ride through the ups and downs of the market. Buy only bonds rated by Moody's or Standard & Poor. And take time to shop around—fees and commissions vary widely from one broker to another. Most mark up the price of the bond and in addition charge for the currency exchange. Many have high minimum purchase requirements, such as $25,000.

Caution: If you do purchase bonds directly, be aware that many countries with high yields, such as Italy and New Zealand, have bonds that are fairly illiquid—meaning that the bonds may be difficult and expensive to sell back to the broker. That's why it's important to hold until maturity.

Hint: To determine which bonds to buy, check the individual Country Market Watch reports in Part Four.

BEFORE BUYING INDIVIDUAL BONDS

1) *Check the maturity date.* The longer the period until a bond matures, generally the higher the yield. On the other hand, your money is tied up—a negative if interest rates rise. Your money is locked in at the old rate, and if you sell during this period, you will do so at a loss because the price of the bond will have fallen.

2) *Check the call date.* Some bonds have what is known as a call provision—the issuer can call in the bond from the investor before the stated maturity date. Protect yourself by purchasing a bond that has call protection: It cannot be called before a stated date. When bonds are called, investors lose their steady stream of interest income and must invest the money either in new bonds with lower yields or elsewhere in the market. (Note: Issuers tend to call bonds when interest rates drop because they can issue new bonds with lower rates, thus reducing their expenses.)

CHAPTER EIGHT

INVESTING FOR GROWTH: FOREIGN STOCK FUNDS

We've already discussed in Chapter 3 how to buy foreign stocks that trade in this country on American Depository Receipts. Yet not all foreign stocks are available through ADRs. One way to tap into the huge non-ADR foreign stock market is through mutual funds. Although you can purchase some foreign stocks on your own through large brokerage firms, it's expensive, time-consuming, and difficult; and some foreign countries don't permit outside investors. Mutual funds are a much easier solution: They handle complicated tax provisions for U.S. investors, hedge against currency fluctuations, and are managed by experts. In 1993 they posted impressive returns: The average world equity fund rose 43 percent; the thirty-seven funds that focus on the Pacific Basin were up an average of 63.8 percent and the nine Latin American funds 57.1 percent—all easily topping the S&P 500's return of 10.1 percent, with dividends reinvested.

1

TOP FOREIGN MUTUAL FUNDS BY CATEGORY

Category	Top Fund/Telephone	Load%
Pacific Rim Asian[1]	**Morgan Stanley Inst.** (800) 548-7786	none
Latin America	**Scudder Latin America** (800) 225-2470	none
International Emerging Mkt[1]	**Morgan Stanley Inst.** (800) 548-7786	none
Global Small Cap	**Prudential Global Genesis A** (800) 225-1852	5.25
Canada	**Mackenzie Canada** (800) 777-6472	5.75
Global	**GAM Global** (800) 888-4200	5.00
Europe	**Dean Witter Europe Growth** (800) 869-3863	redemption
Japan	**GT Japan Growth** (800) 824-1580	4.75

1. Minimum investment: $500,000

INTERNATIONAL STOCK FUNDS

Here's what you need to know to weed out the best funds for 1995–96.

Unlike global funds, which buy shares of foreign and U.S. stocks, these funds focus entirely on foreign securities. The four largest funds in this group are **EuroPacific Growth, T. Rowe Price International Stock, Templeton Foreign,** and **Harbor International**. And, within the international fund category there are many variations. There are those that invest in specific areas, such as **Fidelity Europe Fund** and **G. T. Japan Growth;** those that combine areas, such as the **EuroPacific Growth;** and those that invest around the world, such as the **T. Rowe Price International Stock Fund.** Others focus on emerging countries—in 1993, for instance, Fidelity's **Emerging Markets** was up 81.8 percent based on a portfolio that held stocks in thirty countries, with heavy investments in foreign utility companies, including Telecom Malaysia and Hong Kong Electric as well as many infrastructure stocks. The **Dean Witter European Growth,** which has large positions in Sweden and Norway, has outperformed most Europe-stock funds over the past several years. (See Part Four, Country Spotlights for specific recommendations.)

BENEFITS

1) Because they invest outside the United States, they offer a way to protect money from major declines in the U.S. stock market.
2) Stocks somewhere in the world at any given time are appreciating, and these funds give you a way to participate.
3) They can provide investors a currency advantage.

DRAWBACKS

1) There is an exposure to currency risk: If the U.S. dollar rises, the value of international funds declines.
2) A narrowly focused international fund, such as one that invests in a single country, may not be sufficiently diversified. You could wind up a big loser—or winner.

GLOBAL STOCK FUNDS

Unlike international funds, which do not invest in U.S. stocks, global funds are hybrids and may buy shares of foreign *and* U.S. companies. They may specialize in small companies, in emerging countries, or in blue-chip stocks. Or, they may have no specific limitations and instead seek the top performers or best buys throughout the world. **GAM Global**, with a 5 percent load, and **Prudential Global General A**, which invests in U.S. stocks and stocks in the Far East, with a 5.25 percent load.

BENEFITS

1) They provide wide diversification, wider than international funds, because they can include U.S. stocks.

2) They have less currency risk: Because they are invested in a number of different countries at one time, including the United States, these funds have less currency risk than their international or regional cousins, where the focus is on only one country or area.

   Fund managers move money to take advantage of currency swings: If the dollar is moving up, the portfolio will be dollar denominated; when the dollar declines, the portfolio is shifted to overseas equities.

3) They serve as a hedge or cushion against a decline in the U.S. stock market, but not as much, obviously, as international funds.

DRAWBACKS

1) They may be insufficiently diversified. Too much of your money may be invested in the U.S. market, and if that market drops so will your returns. (Check the prospectus to determine what percentage of a global fund's portfolio is domestically invested.)

2) If the value of the dollar rises, the value of a global fund will decline.

One of the oldest global funds, **New Perspective Fund**, celebrated its twenty-first birthday in 1994. It has had an average return of 14 percent annually over the past five years, built upon a low-turnover growth-oriented portfolio consisting primarily of large-cap stocks. It does not emphasize country weightings or managing currency risks. It keeps about 25 to 33 percent of its assets in the United States and the rest of the focus is on the U.K., Germany, and southeast Asia. In 1994, it had 20 percent of its assets in telecommunication and telephone industries and media companies.

A different approach, one called a "top down" asset allocation approach, is taken by **Putnam Global Growth Fund**. The portfolio manager seeks undervalued mid- and large-cap stocks around the world. It has some 80 percent of its assets invested outside the United States. Over the past five years the fund has averaged 11.7 percent annually. The fund actively hedges currencies. Its Class A shares, which are not subject to a back-end load, also have a lower expense ratio than Class B shares. An interesting new arrival on the scene, **Calvert World Values Fund**, is the first fund that combines a global investment scope with investments in environmentally and socially responsible companies throughout the world. (The Calvert Group is one of the leading mutual-fund companies in the "socially responsible" mutual-fund category.) The fund, launched in the summer of 1992, invests only in companies that are financially promising and act responsibly toward their customers, employees, and the communities in which they operate. It selects companies whose operations, products, and/or services have a positive impact upon the environment, health-care issues, and human rights and therefore avoids companies with significant involvement in nuclear power, the manufacture of weapons systems, and alcohol or tobacco. Among its holdings are:

- **Sodexho.** Largest French company in institutional catering; has excellent employee benefits; recycles materials and holds a forum annually to allow employees to share ideas.

- **Tomra.** A Norwegian manufacturer of machines installed in supermarkets to receive returned bottles and cans, identify them, and calculate refund and return cash to the customer.
- **Pacific Dunlop.** One of Australia's fastest-growing companies; about 25 percent of revenues come from health-care products—surgical gloves, condoms, pacemakers.
- **Toto.** Largest Japanese manufacturer of bathroom fixtures; produces water-efficient toilets, baths and system kitchens. A leader in water conservation technology, the company has no debt.

An interesting fund that covers it all is the **Blanchard Global Growth Fund.** Unlike most mutual funds, which limit their portfolios to a single market or type of investment, this fund pursues growth and income opportunities in six global markets: U.S. stocks, U.S. bonds, foreign stocks, foreign bonds, precious metals, and the securities of the emerging market countries (in Latin America and Asia, primarily). As markets change, so does the composition of the fund through asset allocation by one of the fund's portfolio managers. (Asset allocation is just another way of saying diversification, but in the case of an asset allocation fund, the diversification and proportions of the investments are continually monitored.)

2

TOP GLOBAL EQUITY FUNDS

Fund/Telephone	Sales Fee%	1993 Total Return%
GAM Global (212) 888-4200	5.00	75.30
Prudential Global Genesis A (800) 225-1852	5.25	61.00
Keystone American Global Opportunities A (800) 343-2989	5.75	37.71
Templeton Global Opportunities (800) 237-0738	5.75	30.18
Templeton Growth (800) 237-0738	5.75	25.07
Templeton Smaller Growth Companies (800) 237-0738	5.75	24.27
SMALLCAP World (800) 421-0180	5.75	30.40

3

TIPTOEING THROUGH FOREIGN TULIPS

Both international and global funds buy foreign equities because they are required to do so. Yet there's a less obvious way to go abroad—through a handful of domestic growth equity funds that elect to buy foreign stocks because they wish to, not because it is part of their mandate. **Govett Smaller Companies**, for example, can invest up to 100 percent in foreign stocks if it wishes. It has about a 5 percent position in Canada and Chile, the rest in the United States.

Fund/Telephone	Sales (%)	% Assets Abroad	Foreign Focus	1993 Total Return(%)
Govett Smaller Companies (800) 634-6838	4.95	5	Canada, Chile	58.50
Schafer Value (800) 343-0481	none	12	Mexico, Spain	24.00
Fidelity Value (800) 544-8888	none	19	Japan, U.K.	22.94
Janus Mercury (800) 525-3713	none	15.6	Germany, Chile	19.80
Lindner Fund (314) 727-5305	none	21.9	Europe, Chile	19.85
T. Rowe Price Growth Stock (800) 638-5660	none	20	Europe, Far East	15.56

4

TOP TEN FOREIGN EQUITY FUNDS FOR 1993 (EXCLUDING PACIFIC REGION FUNDS)

Fund	1993 Total Return(%)
Morgan Stanley Instit Emerging Mkts	85.81
Fidelity Emerging Markets	81.76
GAM International	79.97
Govett Emerging Markets	79.73
Templeton Developing Markets	74.50
Merrill Developing Capital Markets	68.96
GT Global Emerging Markets A	64.46
Lexington Worldwide Emerging Markets	63.37
Montgomery Emerging Markets	58.66
Govett International Equity	54.50

5

TOP EIGHT PACIFIC REGION FUNDS FOR 1993

Fund	1993 Total Return(%)
Morgan Stanley Instit Asian Equity	105.71
Dean Witter Pacific Growth	94.71
Merrill Dragon Fund A	87.16
Merrill Dragon Fund B	85.75
Wright Equity Hong Kong	84.32
Eaton Vance China Growth	80.75
T. Rowe Price Int'l Asian	78.76
World Funds Newport Tiger	75.37

CHAPTER NINE

CLOSED-END FOREIGN STOCK AND BOND FUNDS

There are well over 3,000 open-end mutual funds—a daunting thought if there ever was one, but there are only about 600 of the closed-end variety. Even that's an awesome number. Of these, just about 100 invest in foreign countries. Most invest in a specific country, hence the name "country funds." There are also closed-end regional and global funds as well as small cap funds. ("Small cap" generally refers to corporations that do less than $200 million in annual sales.) Unlike open-end funds, which issue new shares on a continual basis, closed-end funds, also known as "publicly traded funds," sell a fixed number of shares to the public only once, in what is called an initial public offering (IPO). This IPO takes place when the fund is launched. Because of this one-time sale, these funds have a fixed capitalization. (With open-end funds, the capitalization continually fluctuates as investors purchase and redeem their shares.) Once the IPO is completed, closed-end funds do not isssue additional shares. Nor do they redeem old ones, as is the case with open-end funds. Instead, shares trade on the stock exchanges or over the counter in the secondary market as common stocks, and investors buy and sell those shares through a stockbroker. The amount of commission is based upon the number of shares traded and whether it is through a discount or full-service broker.

Like open-end funds, closed-end funds offer diversification and professional management. Here, the similarities end. With closed-end funds the NAV is not the sole basis for determining the per share price. Because these funds trade as stocks, their shares are priced either above the NAV, at a premium, or below the NAV, at a discount. For example, a fund with a NAV of $10, selling at $12 per share, is said to be trading at a 20 percent premium. The NAV and share price for the majority of funds are listed in the financial press. (See box.)

When the funds are initially offered in an IPO, they invariably sell at a premium of about 7 percent over their NAV. This premium is due to the underwriting costs the investment company incurs—fees paid to a sponsor and commissions to brokers who sell the funds to customers. These costs are actually built into the price of the shares.

After their initial offering, prices for the funds generally fall to a discount to NAV. Two things to be learned from this scenario: One, don't buy from a broker pushing an IPO, and two, buy in the secondary market at a discount; then, if the share price appreciates, you can sell at a profit. Shares are likely to trade at a premium if the fund invests in companies in countries or geographical areas that are regarded as "hot." There are various types of closed-end funds, investing in U.S. stocks, bonds, utilities, and so on, but here we are focusing on those that invest in foreign stocks, commonly referred to as country funds, or, if they invest in only one country, such as the **Italy Fund** or the **Mexico Fund**, as single country funds.

WHEN TO BUY

- The best time is to buy when a fund is selling at a discount to NAV, in particular when it's near its largest discount (or smallest premium). You then can make money on any rise in share price.

- When fund prices fall—generally six to eight weeks after the underwriting.
- December is typically a good time to buy because investors are selling holdings for tax purposes, and prices tend to fall slightly.
- Just before a rights offer expires; these dilute the value of shares.
- When negative international news or economic events push down the prices of foreign funds.
- Closed-end funds also are part of what Wall Street calls the "January effect," in which stock prices rise at the beginning of the new year—a good time to sell if you want to take profits.
- Buy immediately after a political or economic event is announced. If you wait too long the price will have moved too much—up on favorable news, down on negative news. For example, when Carlos Salinas de Gortari became Mexico's president in late 1988, he stabilized the currency and curtailed inflation. The Mexican market began climbing and along with it the **Mexico Fund.** The fund's NAV doubled in two years.

BENEFITS

- These funds offer a way to pinpoint invest—if you know you want to be in a specific country, such as Mexico or Ireland.
- When a country restricts foreign investment in local companies or is closed entirely to American investors, these funds are the only way to participate in these stock markets. Closed-end funds are able to fully invest all their capital—unlike open-end funds, they do not have to maintain large cash reserves or sell assets (perhaps at a loss) to meet the demands of shareholders who wish to redeem their shares.

- Because their capital remains constant, they are also well suited for thinly traded and/or illiquid markets. In an open-end fund when the foreign market takes a dive, fund managers have to redeem shares as investors seek to get their money back. Because closed-end funds are traded on the stock market or over the counter, they are not forced to sell holdings to raise cash in such situations.
- In a bull market, managers aren't faced with the problem of investing a huge inflow of cash from new investors.
- They offer a way to make money if you sell shares at a higher price than you paid for them.

DRAWBACKS

- During a bear market, the price of a fund may drop to a deep discount to the NAV.
- Single country funds often react noticeably (and often negatively) to political and economic developments.
- Their portfolios, when limited to a single country or area, are not widely diversified and therefore have a fairly high risk factor.
- Many investors do not focus attention on the premium or discount to NAV factor and are surprised if shares fall in price. When U.S. investors lose interest in a specific foreign market, the country fund typically drops in price.
- You're buying shares of a fund in dollars, but the portfolio of a country fund is denominated in another currency—one that you may be unfamiliar with or too busy to track. If so, you would be wiser to invest in an open-end mutual fund where the portfolio manager is up to date on the country's economy and stocks.

SELECTING A CLOSED-END FUND

There are two ways to make money on country funds—wait
for the securities in the portfolio to rise in value or sell shares
at a higher price than you paid for them. This makes evaluation of funds more complicated than with open-end funds: You
must determine the outlook for the price of the fund as well as
the outlook for the fund's portfolio.

To effectively analyze the portfolio, use the same criteria as
with any investment: How good is management? Does the
fund's investment strategy match your objectives? How well
has the fund performed in the past?

To judge the direction of the price of the shares, as traded
on the stock market, first determine if the stock is selling near
its largest discount. If so, then ask yourself if other investors
will prize the fund and thus push up the price. Making an
accurate assessment is not an easy task, for the market for
country funds moves quickly and share prices are often
volatile, reacting to political and economic events. For
instance, when the Berlin Wall came down, the price of the
Germany Fund soared and at one point was at a premium of
100 percent over NAV, only to tumble to a discount of 15 percent when it became apparent that German unification would
be a slow and expensive process.

Pick a country or region where economic growth is likely to
take place fairly quickly and where stock prices are still relatively low. You can further increase your profit potential by
avoiding countries where there is great political upheaval and
economic instability.

CLONES

As a country's equities grow in popularity, clone funds are
often launched to accommodate the public, eager to invest.
Most clones generally have slightly paler blue-chip holdings
and can be purchased at a discount, at least for a while.

Examples of clones are **The New Germany Fund, The Future Germany Fund, The Emerging Germany Fund, The Emerging Mexican Fund**, and the **Mexican Equity & Income Fund.**

GETTING RESEARCH

Because these funds are sold by stockbrokers, you can ask your broker for research reports by the firm's analysts. A number of leading country funds are also evaluated on a regular basis in *Value Line* and *Morningstar* (see Appendix). You can also contact the fund directly for an annual and quarterly reports.

> *Hint*: For a free brochure listing phone numbers for the funds, call Thomas J. Hertzfield & Co., (516) 791-4444.
> Additional information is dispensed through several newsletters that track closed-end funds. (see Appendix)

Among the country funds selling at a discount as of September 1994 were:

• **Brazil Fund**	-3.9%
• **First Philippine Fund**	-18.2%
• **Growth Fund of Spain**	-13.0%
• **Irish Investment Fund**	-8.5%
• **New Germany Fund**	-16.2%
• **Scudder New Europe**	-12.6%
• **Thai Fund**	-9.0%

Among the country funds selling at a premium as of January 1994 were:

• **China Fund**	+21.0%
• **Indonesia Fund**	+39.3%
• **Japan Equity**	+1.7%
• **Korea Fund**	+16.9%

- **Mexico Fund**   +4.7%
- **Turkish Investment Fund**   +38.9%

Specific country funds are also listed in each of the Country Spotlight sections in Part Four of this book.

CHAPTER TEN

INTERNATIONAL MARKET INDEXES AND INDEX FUNDS

An index seeks to capture in a single number the change in value of an entire market by tracking the performance of a specific group of securities within that market. Whether glancing at a headline or talking with a friend, for most people it is easiest to follow foreign stock markets via the shorthand of an index, such as the Nikkei 225 for Japan, or Morgan Stanley's EAFE Index, composed of stocks in Europe, Australia, and the Far East. Each country has one or more indexes that are the most-watched barometers of its markets. They are invaluable to the U.S. investor attempting to appraise overseas financial opportunities.

WHAT IS AN INDEX FUND?

Index funds are designed by banks, brokerage houses, and fund management companies to produce investment returns that mirror changes in a specific index. A number of mutual funds have been launched with portfolios modeled on the EAFE and other international market indexes. Index mutual funds are often called "passive funds" because the composition of their portfolios is relatively stable. They shift their holdings only when a stock is added to or deleted from the index they are tracking.

WHY BUY AN INDEX FUND?

Because index funds require less buying and selling of stocks than a conventional mutual fund, they represent a cost-effective way to participate in a broad diversification of securities. Most international index funds are less than five years old, but high performance at low cost is strong reason to consider them as a conservative core holding of your international portfolio. A study covering 1981 through 1991, showed that Morgan Stanley's EAFE Index beat the median fund manager performance by almost 1 1/2 percent annually. In four of those years, the index itself scored in the top 5 percent of all foreign stock managers. When you consider how difficult it is for investment fund managers to beat a market index, it is clear that funds designed to track that index should perform relatively well.

HOW TO USE AN INDEX

Indexes allow quick, easy historical comparisons. For example, in the fifteen years ending June 30, 1993, the S&P 500 increased on average 15.6 percent annually, while Morgan Stanley's EAFE Index rose 16.6 percent. Graphing the indexes along with the performance of relevant investment alternatives makes the comparison vivid. Result: We can see that stocks both at home and abroad significantly outperformed U.S. bonds and CDs during the same period.

In addition to being used as a yardstick to evaluate the performance of other investments, an index reflects market trends, showing how the overall market is faring, for better or worse, and to what extent. Comparing indexes from different geographic regions can give you an idea of changing trends in global markets—when and where to shift your investments.

AVERAGE ANNUAL TOTAL RETURNS FOR
15 YEARS ENDING JUNE 30, 1993

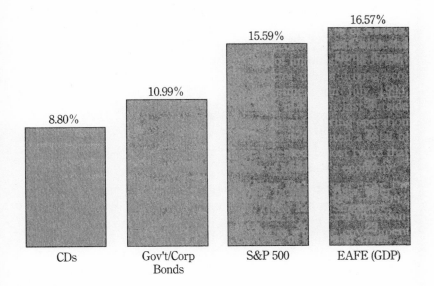

TYPES OF INDEXES

The increase in new indexes that gauge foreign and international stock performance has paralleled the rapid growth of investor interest in global markets. The financial press reports on most of them, using the following categories:

FOREIGN STOCK EXCHANGE INDEXES

These indexes track the performance of a specific group of stocks traded on the stock exchange of a foreign country. They are often the most highly regarded measure of a country's overall equity market and receive extensive news coverage.

- Country indexes assess the broad performance of a country's stocks. Whereas the DAX Index contains only thirty stocks listed on the Frankfurt Exchange, the Dow Jones German Stock Index contains a broader cross selection of stocks listed on exchanges throughout the country.

- Regional indexes track the markets of a specific geographic area, such as Asia-Pacific, Europe, and the Americas.

- International indexes measure the performance of stock markets outside the United States.

- Global indexes evaluate the performance of U.S. and foreign stocks.

- Industry indexes. Whether it's automobiles, advertising, precious metals, or paper products, each has an index of the stocks in its industry, organized globally or by country or region. The *Wall Street Journal*, for example, breaks down its World Index in this way.

Index	Exchange
All Ordinaries	The Australian Stock Exchange
TSE 300	Toronto Stock Exchange (Canada)
CAC 40	Bourse de Paris (France)
DAX Index	Frankfurt Stock Exchange (Germany)
Hang Seng Index	Hong Kong Stock Exchange
MIB Index	Borsa Valori di Milano (Italy)
Nikkei 225, TOPIX	Tokyo Stock Exchange (Japan)
Bolsa	Bolsa Mexicana de Valores (Mexico)
Straits Index	The Stock Exchange of Singapore
SPI	Zurich Stock Exchange (Switzerland)
FTSE-100 ("Footsie Index")	London Stock Exchange (United Kingdom)

THREE INDEXES TO TRACK

Global indexes track investments throughout the world, including U.S. markets, while international indexes measure investments outside the United States. There are international and global indexes that investors should be particularly aware of, either because they are widely followed or because they are used as target investment objectives for foreign mutual funds, or they are good indicators of the direction foreign economies are taking.

THE EAFE (EUROPE AUSTRALIA FAR EAST) INDEX

Morgan Stanley Capital International (MSCI) was the first to provide a diversified international index. MSCI's EAFE is a standard benchmark for many international fund managers. The Vanguard Group offers investors the chance to participate in the European portion of the EAFE or the Asian portion of the index, through the Vanguard International Equity Index Fund, European Portfolio, and Pacific Portfolio. *Hint*: Replicate the whole index by purchasing shares in both.

THE FT WORLD INDEX

The Financial Times (FT) World Indices measure global stock market performance. They are compiled through the joint efforts of the *Financial Times*, Goldman Sachs & Co., and Country NatWest/Wood Mackenzie in conjunction with the U.K.'s Institute of Actuaries and the Faculty of Actuaries. The FT World Indices can be broken down into regions, such as its Europe–Pacific Basin index, and further into country indexes.

THE DOW JONES WORLD INDEX

The Dow Jones World Index was launched on January 5, 1993, by the creator of the Dow Jones Industrial Average, perhaps the best-known index of them all. The Dow Jones World Index is published daily in the *Wall Street Journal*. This world index is now also broken down by industry as well as by region and country. During 1994, a comparison of the auto industry stocks in Europe, Japan, and the United States gave clues as to how their respective economies were doing—in other words, in slow growing, ending recession, and brisk growth.

VARIETIES OF INDEX FUNDS

PURE

A pure index fund would own all the stocks of the index that it is modeled on. Owning them all, however, is often impractical. Some stocks in the EAFE, for example, are not available to U.S. residents, so exactly reproducing that index is impossible.

A NEAR CLONE

Index managers buy a broad selection of stocks that closely mirror their target index. As of 1988, it was estimated that owning 675 of the 957 stocks in the EAFE index was sufficient to replicate the performance of the EAFE, while it took 900 of the 1,620 stocks in the FT's Europe–Pacific Basin Index to duplicate its results. Though not always a perfect match, an index that costs less to purchase and maintain can be more profitable.

PURE VERSUS HYBRID INDEXES

Occasionally a fund will customize an index for use as an investment target. In the late 1980s, Japan's bull market had pumped up stock prices to between forty and sixty times earnings, and index managers felt uncomfortable placing a high portion of international assets there. To get around this, some funds decided to invest in countries according to the relative size of their economies, not on the size of their stock markets alone. At the time, this "GDP-weighting" of the EAFE Index dramatically lowered Japan's share from 60 to 40 percent and cushioned performance somewhat during Japan's bear market.

1

A SLIGHT CHANGE IN HOW AN INTERNATIONAL INDEX IS CONSTRUCTED CAN DRAMATICALLY CHANGE HOW MUCH AN INDEX FUND WILL INVEST IN EACH COUNTRY.

EAFE country weightings

	GDP-weighted EAFE[1] (%)	CAP-weighted EAFE[2] (%)
France	11.10	6.74
Germany	13.31	6.85
Italy	10.08	2.13
Spain	3.82	1.86
United Kingdom	8.55	19.04
Others	*13.05*	*12.19*
Total Europe:	**59.91**	**48.81**
Japan	36.39	43.32
Others	3.69	7.87
Total Pacific:	**40.09**	**51.19**
Total:	**100.00%**	**100.00%**

1. Based on the relative size of each country's Gross Domestic Product.

2. Capitalization-weighted, based on the relative dollar value of each country's stock market.

A FUND THAT ASPIRES TO BEAT THE AVERAGES

Some funds seek to outperform the index they are based on. They invest in only a portion of an index's stocks, depending on which one their research highlights as the most likely winners of the group. **Fidelity's Diversified International Fund**, for example, invests in similar industries as the EAFE Index but not necessarily the same stocks. As of mid-1994, the Fidelity fund owned 315 stocks, compared with more than 900 included in the EAFE. In its short history, so far, it has come close but has not beaten the index.

2
LEADING INTERNATIONAL INDEX FUNDS

Fund Phone	Index Objective
Fidelity Diversified Int'l (800) 544-8888; 1993 total return:	modified EAFE
Vanguard Int'l-Europe (800) 662-7447; 1993 total return:	MSCI Europe
Vanguard Int'l-Pacific (800) 662-7447; 1993 total return:	MSCI Pacific

THE BENEFITS OF INDEX FUNDS

They are 100 percent invested in stocks (or bonds) at all times. Because most equity funds maintain cash reserves of 5 to 10 percent of assets, they have lost ground in the long-term bull market of the past decade.

Caution: In periods of market declines, index funds may underperform funds that maintain cash reserves.

Indexed portfolios have low turnover. Because index funds change the composition of their portfolios only when a stock is added to or deleted from the index they are tracking, they buy and sell less stock than other types of mutual funds, so-called "active funds," which change their portfolios any time they discover a "better" security. It is not unusual for an active fund to turn over 50 to 100 percent of its holdings each year, whereas index funds typically need to adjust less than 15 percent of their holdings annually.

Index funds have the lowest operating costs of any class of mutual fund. Low portfolio activity allows index funds to avoid expensive foreign brokerage commissions. Because a fund's composition is determined by the index that it follows, the cost of an active fund manager with a "major league" salary is unnecessary. Stock turnover in foreign markets is more costly than in the United States for several reasons. Here's a hidden one—wider spreads between foreign bid and offer prices (where you can buy a stock and where you can sell it). Bid/ask spreads in foreign markets average over 1 percent, and can be significantly higher for smaller-capitalized companies in emerging markets. Also, foreign stock exchange taxes run as high as 1 percent of a transaction's value.

Index funds usually charge lower fees. Actively managed international mutual funds have, on the average, costlier front- and back-end "loads" compared with index funds, which makes beating the net performance of the international index funds even harder.

HOW TO CHOOSE AN INTERNATIONAL INDEX FUND

- Compare the results of different funds based on the same index. Compare returns for funds with the same target index that interest you. Choose the fund with the higher, steadier returns.

- Load versus no-load. Expenses are anathema to index funds. The operating methods preclude the need to charge "loads" (fees for buying into and divesting from a fund). International index funds are relatively new, however, and some have gotten away with charging fees as high as any actively managed funds, 3 percent or more in some cases. *There is no reason to choose them.* On the other hand, the field *is* still new. Do not avoid a fund with a low-load that targets exactly the index you want.

- Review the operating expenses. Read the prospectus carefully. Choose an international index fund with the lowest operating costs. Review a fund's operating expenses, particularly new ones. While the ongoing costs of running an index fund are low, there are one-time setup costs—but newer funds should pro-rate these expenses over the estimated life of the fund.

- Compare the fund's results to the target index. Call the toll-free number and ask a sales representative for the fund's up-to-date performance data and information on how the index itself did during that time. If the information is not easy to find in the prospectus, the comparison probably does not favor the fund. The historical performance of a market index does not include the expenses a fund has to pay. Still, it is better to avoid funds that consistently underperform their target index by 2 percent or more.

Hint: For higher returns, consider selecting a fund that targets a particular country or region that you think will outperform the others. A narrow geographic bet can increase your upside potential by focusing on a "hot" area. Within that region or country you participate in a broad group of stocks. Not surprisingly, the prospect of higher returns comes with the risk of that region eventually underperforming. Be nimble about shifting back to a broader geographic region when you think the trend is losing steam.

WHEN TO GET OUT

- If another fund tracking the same index turns in a consistently better performance, consider switching to it.
- Watch expenses as a percent of fund assets. The job of an index fund is to track its target index at the lowest cost possible. If expenses rise it could mean management problems—they're either not running a tight ship or have decided to soak the shareholders!
- If the index you choose meets your profit objectives, review your reasons for staying with it. Ask yourself, "Would I buy it today?" If the answer is not, "Yes,"

then liquidate. If there is a region of the globe you think will significantly outperform the one you are in, then switch.

3
AN INTERESTING NEW INDEX FUND

In late 1993, Charles Schwab & Co. launched an index fund designed to track its new index—the Schwab International Index. The index measures the performance of the 350 largest publicly traded companies outside the United States, representing nearly half the international marketplace, based on market capitalization. This no-load fund should be an efficient way to diversify investments abroad. Phone: (800) 435-4000.

IV

THE GLOBAL MARKETPLACE:
WHO'S HOT AND WHO'S NOT

CHAPTER ELEVEN

COUNTRY SPOTLIGHTS AND OVERVIEWS

ARGENTINA

Buy

INVESTMENT FACTORS

	1993	1994E
Real Economic Growth:	6.0%	5.0%
Inflation:	8.0%	8.0%
Current Account (% of GDP):	-8.0%	-9.0%

Political: Argentina has a stable government. President Carlos Saul Menem runs an authoritarian brand of democracy that has popular support because it has fostered strong economic growth.

STOCK MARKET OUTLOOK

After this market advanced 55 percent—in U.S. dollars—in 1993, it came as no surprise that it took a breather. Argentine equities will continue, however, to be above-average performers, as global institutional investors diversifying choose this market for its political stability and growth prospects. Economic output continues to expand at a healthy pace, and inflation, at less than 10 percent, will remain relatively moderate. No change is expected in the country's policy of pegging its currency, the Austral, to the U.S. dollar.

STOCKS TO CONSIDER
- **Buenos Aires Embottelledora S.A.** (NYSE: BAE) Earnings keep growing at this soft-drink company which is 35 percent owned by Pepsi.
- **Telefonica de Argentina** (NASDAQ: TFOBF) The national phone company has healthy long-term prospects as demand for phones is expanding faster than growth in this vigorous economy.
- **YPF Sociedad Anonmia** (NYSE: YPF) Previously the state-owned energy company, YPF was 1993's largest global privatization, worth nearly $3 billion. Oil and natural gas production is expected to increase, and the company will benefit from increased efficiencies.

A CLOSED-END FUND

- **The Argentina Fund** (NYSE: AF) This fund provides a diversified play on the Argentine stock market. It earned 42.5 percent in 1993, lower than the overall market, because of its cash holdings. Its largest holdings are the three companies, whose ADRs are listed directly above, which made up 16.32 percent of the fund's holdings.

OVERVIEW

Argentina's economy is one of the success stories other emerging nations are trying to emulate. What's astonishing is not just the magnitude of the change that has occurred but also the speed at which Argentina turned itself around. Not long ago Argentina's economy was a picture of what didn't work in South America—democracy in shambles, a declining economy, hyperinflation, increasing external debt, and a shaky currency.

HOW ARGENTINA PUT ITS ECONOMIC HOUSE IN ORDER

In 1989, President Carlos Menem took office, and his government quickly passed measures that deregulated industry, introduced fiscal and monetary control, and began what became an extensive privatization of government-owned industry.

The results have been dramatic.

- Inflation was running at 6,000 percent annually when President Menem took office in 1989; it was running 10 percent in 1994.

- The economy has averaged economic growth of almost 9 percent each year since 1991—the highest growth rate in South America.

- Almost all of the government-owned businesses have been sold, including railroads, the telephone company, electric utilities, and the state oil company, and proceeds have gone to pay off the country's external debt.

- In 1991, Argentina's stock market acknowledged the impact of reforms and soared 405 percent—in dollars.

ARGENTINA'S STOCK MARKET

The Stock Exchange of Buenos Aires was established in 1854, making it the oldest in Latin America. Market performance is measured by the Merval Index of nineteen blue-chip stocks, which account for 80 percent of the trading volume there.

ARGENTINA HAS A STABLE CURRENCY

In 1991, Argentina pegged its currency, the Austral, to the dollar. When the value of the dollar increases or decreases compared with other currencies, the Austral is adjusted by the same percentage. A stable Austral has reduced the uncertainty of large currency price movements and has therefore stimulated trade and increased investor confidence.

BOND HOLDERS HAVE PROFITED

Before President Menem, Argentina's debt was unrated; it did not even merit a "junk bond" investment rating from Moody's Investors Services. In 1991, based upon improved economic results, Moody's Investors Services gave Argentina's national bonds a B3 rating, their lowest investment grade. By June 1992, though, Argentina's bonds skipped two rating categories to a B1 rating. The good news for bond investors was that, as Argentina's credit rating improved, investors perceived that its bonds were less risky, so Argentina's bonds increased in price, providing profits to the bond holders.

AUSTRALIA

Buy

INVESTMENT FACTORS

	1993	*1994E*
Real Economic Growth:	2.5%	4.0%
Inflation:	2.0%	2.0%
Current Account (% of GDP):	-3.5%	-3.0%
3-month A$ deposits:	5.0%	5.0%
10-year bond yields:	7.5%	8.0%

Economy: Growth in the economies of southeast Asia will benefit Australia, as will continued low interest rates. Expect Australia's growth to proceed as in the United States; steady, not sensational.

STOCK MARKET OUTLOOK

Australia's equities should continue higher in 1995, partly because of rising expectations that global inflation will increase. Though inflation is expected to remain dormant, this may not hold true in late 1995 as the world's economies expand and spare industrial capacity gets used up. Because stocks prices discount the probabilities of such events, hold onto shares in Australia's natural resource companies to profit from the rising expectation that inflation will pick up late in 1994 and throughout 1995.

STOCKS TO CONSIDER:

- **Broken Hill Pty.** (NYSE: BHP) Australia's largest company has been turning in higher profits from its domestic natural resource operations and has good long-term prospects globally. For instance, it is developing oil in Vietnam and exploring for minerals in Africa and diamonds in Canada.
- **CocaCola Amatyle** (OTC) Has the franchise to bottle and distribute Coca-Cola in Australia, New Zealand, Indonesia, the Czech Republic, and Hungary.
- **News Corp.** (NYSE: NWS) News Corp. is on the cutting edge of broadcasting and technology and is expanding into the world's emerging economies. For instance, in 1993 it bought

66 percent of Star Television, Hong Kong, and formed a joint venture in Mexico with the dominant television company there, Grupo Televisa.
- **Pacific Dunlop** (NASDAQ: PDLPY) This consumer conglomerate has sold off money-losing divisions, has rising profits from its core operations, and has its sights set on sales to foreign markets.

A CLOSED-END AUSTRALIAN FUND
- **First Australian** (ASE: IAF) This fund was loaded with natural resource stocks that propelled it ahead 69.6 percent for 1993, by far surpassing the overall market's 38 percent gain.

CLOSED-END AUSTRALIAN BOND FUNDS	1994 YIELD
• **First Australia** **Prime Income** (ASE: FAX)	9.6%
• **Kleinwort Benson** **Australian Income** (NYSE: KBA)	7.8%

OVERVIEW

Don't overlook the land Down Under when considering how to benefit from Asia's growth. Slightly smaller than the United States, Australia has immense natural resources and only 18 million people (compared with the United States' 260 million). Its economy is prosperous with a per capita GDP similar to those of industrialized west European countries. More than 70 percent of Australia's trade is with the rapidly growing economies of Asia, and as those countries grow, they are going to import a lot more of what Australia has to offer, which includes the following.
- Enormous mineral resources—abundant bauxite deposits (the

basic ingredient for aluminum), increasing amounts of iron ore (used in making steel), as well as zinc, lead, nickel, and copper.

- Significant coal and energy supplies. At double the present consumption rates, Australia's coal, natural gas, and oil reserves will last 100 to 200 years.

- One of the world's foremost agricultural exporters, Australia leads the world in wool production and is an important supplier of wheat and other grains, dairy products, meat, sugar, and fruit.

THE AUSTRALIAN EQUITIES MARKET

The Australian Stock Exchange is a combination of stock markets in six cities throughout Australia, though Sydney and Melbourne account for 90 percent of the trading volume. The All Ordinaries Index is the market's broadest performance measure. Rising prices of gold and other natural resources give a strong underpinning to the market. American individuals and institutions own nearly $4 billion worth of Australia's equities.

BOND AND CURRENCY OUTLOOK

Australian bond funds should continue to do well in 1995, with stable, high yields and a steady to firmer Australian dollar. The Aussie dollar ended 1993 at U.S. $.6750, down 2.5 percent from the year earlier. With an improving economy and the country's raw materials increasing in price, the A-dollar firmed up in 1994 and traded well over $.70, providing currency gains to foreign investors.

AN INFLATION HEDGE

An upturn in the global economy can have a big impact on Australia and its stock market. Twenty-one of the country's top twenty-five exports are natural resource–based or bulk agricultural products. Australia's exports provide the raw materials needed for economic growth in Asia and elsewhere in the world. When the economies of its trading partners expand, Australian exports typically increase in quantity. When inflation occurs, the price of Australia's raw materials go up, and the total value of Australia's exports increases. Weighted with natural resource companies, the Australian stock market is a hedge against inflation because these companies show increased profits during periods of price inflation.

BRAZIL

Hold

INVESTMENT FACTORS

	1993	1994E
Real Economic Growth:	4%	3%
Inflation:	@ 2500%	@ 1000%
Current Account (% of GDP):	0.7%	0.5%

Political: Unfortunately, former President Collor was not the only one stealing from the government's coffers; 1993 revealed that much of the elected legislature had siphoned off large sums. The military has threatened to intervene if the government does not mend its ways, and, in Brazil, the threat of military coup is not an idle one. That makes Brazil a high-risk bet.

STOCK MARKET OUTLOOK

As of December 1993, the Brazilian market was up nearly 100 percent for the year—in U.S. dollars. Investors considering Brazil need to put those gains into perspective.

Consider how discouraging the political climate was at year end 1992, after the impeachment of Brazil's president. Brazilian equities were selling at half to one-third their book value and at seven or eight times the level of 1992's depressed earnings. Although contrarians profited in 1993 as the market rallied from oversold conditions, today caution is in order for 1994–95 as Brazil's current economic and political challenges are immense.

ONE BRAZILIAN STOCK TO CONSIDER

- **Telebras** (OTC: TBRAY) Brazil's telephone monopoly is perhaps the cheapest phone company in an emerging market. At $35, it is selling below book value and has a single-digit P/E ratio. Expect volatile price moves; the country's largest company reacts in line with changes in investor sentiment toward Brazil, which occur often.

CLOSED-END BRAZIL FUNDS
- **Brazil Fund** (NYSE: BZF)   +61.9% in 1993
- **Brazilian Equity** (NYSE: BZL)   +73.4% in 1993

CLOSED-END REGIONAL FUNDS THAT INVEST IN BRAZIL

	1993 Returns	% of Assets in Brazil
• **Latin American Discovery** (NYSE: LDF)	104.7%	40
• **Latin America Equity** (NYSE: LAQ)	88.4%	25

OVERVIEW

Brazil is the largest country in South America and by far the most populous, with 160 million people. Brazil's economy has mouth-watering potential, based on its superlative mineral resources, agriculture, and manufacturing infrastructure. In fact, its economy is the eighth largest in the world.

Brazil has two main stock exchanges: São Paulo (the Bovespa), which accounts for two-thirds of the trading volume, and the Stock Exchange of Rio de Janeiro. Over the years, the market's performance has mirrored Brazil's volatile economic performance. Indeed, with hyperinflation of 30 percent a month, South America's giant remains a sobering reminder of the continent's former problems of economic stagnation and colossal debt.

POLITICAL INSTABILITY

Economic momentum has been stalled by political corruption, best evidenced by the 1992 impeachment of President Collor de Mello because of his theft of millions of dollars from the government.

Confidence in elected officials has not improved since then, and there has been talk of a return of the military, which controlled the government from 1964 until 1985. Justified or not, the region's predilection for strongman governments and coup-meisters is associated with past defaults, which is why Brazilian political turmoil depresses stock prices there.

BRAZIL'S CURRENCY IS LOOSELY LINKED TO THE DOLLAR

Brazil seems to put out new currencies faster than the Chicago Bulls win championships. As of 1994, though, Brazil indirectly linked its currency to the dollar. Monetary authorities there are keeping Brazilian short-term interest rates 10 to 20 percent higher than the rate at which their currency depreciates against the dollar. This is an unwritten policy, which could be changed at any time, but it reflects the acknowledgment by Brazil's Treasury and Central Bank that foreign investors must be well compensated for the risk of placing deposits in Brazilian money markets.

AN INVESTMENT STRATEGY

- Stay away from owning individual Brazilian stocks. Limit your investment choices to mutual funds that specialize in Brazil or a Latin American fund that owns Brazilian stocks. Take advantage of the professional investment selection and diversification afforded by such funds.
- Buy only when the Brazilian market experiences one of its frequent losing streaks. For instance, watch the closed-end funds listed above; consider buying if they go down in price 20 percent to 40 percent. Sound extreme? It is, but investing in Brazil is still risky. The country's potential is as large as its failings.

CAN TODAY'S INVESTOR GET TARRED AS THE BANKS DID IN THE 1980S?

No doubt Brazil's economic performance will be volatile as long as its political system remains chaotic. Investors considering Brazil have an additional hurdle to confront, because it has not eliminated the problems, such as hyperinflation, that culminated in the Latin debt crisis of a decade ago.

Diversifying is the key for most investors hoping to make money in Brazil. Unless you have reason to believe that a particular company or industry will significantly outperform the rest, spread your holdings across several industries by owning shares in a mutual fund that specializes in Brazil or a Latin American fund that has Brazilian holdings. Mutual-fund managers can shift holdings to take advantage of better investment prospects, take profits, or get rid of a loss. That is essential to the individual investor because there will be losers—individual stock performance in Brazil will be more erratic than in the United States for years to come.

Perhaps the best news of all for today's investor is that the region has spawned economic success stories, such as Chile and Argentina, that have relatively well-regulated stock markets and above-average economic growth—those are examples Brazilians would like to emulate.

CANADA

Buy

INVESTMENT FACTORS

	1993	1994E
Real Economic Growth:	2.5%	4.0%
Inflation:	2.0%	2.0%
Current Account (% of GDP):	-3.5%	-2.5%
3-month C$ deposits:	5.0%	5.0%
10-year bond yields:	7.3%	8.0%

Political: In the last election, Jean Chretien's Liberal Party trounced the incumbent Conservatives, taking 177 of the 295 seats. Chretien swiftly gave his approval to NAFTA, and his star has been rising.

STOCK MARKET OUTLOOK

Canada's economy should pick up steam as the United States' does and will profit from growth in the economies of its other trading partners.

STOCKS TO CONSIDER

- **Bank of Montreal** (TSE: BMO.TO) Canada's third-largest bank reported record profits for 1993, the fourth year in a row, and higher earnings are expected in 1995. The bank is expanding strongly in the United States through Harris Bankcorp., which it owns.
- **Canadian Pacific** (NYSE: CP) Involved in all aspects of Canada's economy, CP is an appealing long-term holding that will benefit from NAFTA.
- **Labatt** (TSE: LBT.TO) This Canadian beer producer's market share has expanded to 44.6 percent of the domestic market, and it has an increasing presence in the United States.
- **Seagram's** (NYSE: VO) Earnings may advance 20 percent in 1995. Currently 75 percent of its sales are in the United States, but the company's expansion plans overseas are the key to this long-term buy.

OPEN-ENDED MUTUAL FUND TOTAL RETURNS

	1-Year	3-Year	5-Year
• Fidelity Canada:	25.5%	11.6%	10.8%

A NORTH AMERICAN INCOME FUND

Dean Witter markets an open-ended mutual fund, the **North American Government Income Trust,** which is run by Trust Company of the West (TC West), which invests up to 25 percent of the fund's assets in Mexican Treasury Bills. Up to 10 percent of the fund's assets can be invested in Canadian government bills, with the balance in U.S. government–guaranteed securities. The fund's blended yield was 7.23 percent in 1994. The fund's number is: (800) 526-3143, or (800) 869-3863.

OVERVIEW

You do not have to cross an ocean to become an international investor. Canada's markets are similar enough to ours that you can use the same investment analysis to invest there as you would here. Several major American brokerage firms have offices "north of the border" and provide straightforward market access. The Toronto Stock Exchange trades more than three-quarters of Canada's equities, and its TSE 300 Composite Index is the standard by which Canada's stock market is measured. Though the Canadian and U.S. economies are closely linked, Canada's has special characteristics that give it distinct profit opportunities.

- Eighty percent of Canada's exports are shipped to the United States. We are Canada's largest customer. When we do well, Canada also benefits. The reverse can cause swings the other way, and it has spawned the saying "When the U.S. sneezes, Canada catches a cold."

- Canada has vast supplies of natural resources, which gives it good, long-range growth potential. This also acts as a hedge against commodity price inflation.

BOND MARKET OUTLOOK

A strengthening currency and stable interest rates will likely make Canadian bonds a profitable investment through 1995. The potential stumbling block is the unwieldy federal and provincial debt. Parliament has to bring it under control and will likely do so because the bond-rating agencies have become stern watchdogs. Standard & Poor's Corp. downgraded Ontario's debt in 1993. Check current rating before investing.

CURRENCY OUTLOOK

At 72 or 73 cents the Canadian dollar is undervalued, but expect it to stabilize after the Quebec elections in November 1994. Then it should head higher against the U.S. dollar.

THE CANADIAN DOLLAR IS RELATIVELY STABLE

On a historical basis, the Canadian dollar is the least risky currency of our major trading partners. For the past twenty years it has fluctuated between U.S. $.6850 and $1.08, on average staying well within a ten-cent range each year.

Hint: Generally speaking, you have a good chance to add 5 to 10 percent to your investment return if you buy a Canadian stock with Canadian dollars after the currency takes a bashing, such as in 1994, after a three-year decline from 90 to 71 cents.

YOU CAN INVEST WITH U.S. DOLLARS IN CANADIAN COMPANIES

More than 125 Canadian companies are listed on both the TSE and U.S. exchanges (for example, **Cominco** [ASE: CLT], **Seagram's** [NYSE: VO], and **Canadian Pacific** [NYSE: CP]). Five Canadian companies are even included in the U.S. Standard & Poor's 500 Index. There are enough Canadian stocks and bonds denominated in U.S. dollars that you do not have to own Canadian dollars to participate in the growth of the Canadian economy.

PROVINCE, FEDERAL, AND CULTURAL RIGHTS

Canada's provinces have stronger rights than our states, and the country is still grappling with the separation of provincial and federal powers, as well as language and cultural rights of its "two founding peoples"—English and French. When this tug-of-war gets vitriolic, Canada's equities and its currency tend to suffer. Bloc Quebecois is the latest in a series of leading political parties in Quebec that want the province to secede from Canada.

> *Hint*: If the separatist issue causes a pullback in Canadian markets, it could be a buying opportunity for foreign investors, as it was in May 1980, when Quebecuers resoundingly defeated a referendum on self-rule and Canada's markets rallied decisively.

SOLID GROWTH AND A LARGE DEBT BURDEN

Canada's Gross Domestic Product grew nearly 3 percent in 1993 and is expected to outperform the other Group of Seven industrial countries in 1994-1995. However, the high level of provincial and federal borrowings has caused Moody's and Standard & Poor's Corp. to lower their rating on some Canadian long-term debt; that is one reason the Canadian dollar fell throughout 1994. It now takes almost one-third of every Canadian tax dollar to service its debt compared with a quarter of every dollar in the United States.

CHILE

Buy

INVESTMENT FACTORS

	1993	1994E
Real Economic Growth:	6%	5%
Inflation:	13%	12%
Current Account (% of GDP):	- 5%	- 3%

Political: Chileans gave a vote of confidence to their government in December 1993 by electing Eduardo Frei as president, a member of the previous governing coalition, which was well respected for its economic achievements.

STOCK MARKET OUTLOOK

Throughout the country there is a commitment to modernize technology and infrastructure facilities. With improved prices for copper, Chile's economy is expected to grow modestly in 1995. The current account deficit is higher than it has been since 1986, but foreign investment inflows will help fund this and the economy's expansion, which should contribute to higher stock prices.

STOCKS TO CONSIDER

- **Compania Cervecerias** (NASDAQ: CCUUY) This company has 90 percent of Chile's beer market and 30 percent of the soft-drink market. Expect it to benefit from a growing economy.
- **Maderas y Sinteticos** (NYSE: MYS) The firm makes 95 percent of the world's particle board, an important construction material. From furniture to houses, it's used throughout Chile's expanding economy.
- **Telefonos de Chile** (NYSE: CTC) Provides 95 percent of Chile's local telephone services. Sales to the business clientele is running more than 25 percent per year, with steadily rising profits.

A CLOSED-END FUND

- **The Chile Fund** (NYSE: CH) This fund provides a diversified play on Chile's stock market. It has been profitable each year since it began in September 1989, providing returns, on average, of more than 40 percent annually.

REGIONAL CLOSED-END FUNDS THAT INVEST IN CHILE

	1993 Returns	% of Assets in Chile
• **Latin America Equity** (NYSE, LAQ)	88.4%	22
• **Latin America Investment** (NYSE, LAM)	76.9%	20

OVERVIEW

Chile is little more than 100 miles wide yet stretches 2,600 miles down the west coast of South America from Peru to the southern end of the continent. It has the most stable politics and economy in South America. Since the early 1970s it has been applying free-market principles to its economy, and investors have been reaping the benefits.

- From 1985 through 1990, the thirty most active stocks gained 79 percent each year, in dollars.
- Copper is Chile's number-one export. In 1982, Chile overtook the United States to become the leading producer of the metal. Other mineral resources and a diversified manufacturing base provide the foundation for the Chilean economy.

A New Economic Standard

Economic momentum has been brisk as a mix of policies has lowered inflation, balanced the budget, streamlined government, lowered tariffs, and deregulated industry. Chile's economy averaged a 6 percent growth rate from 1986 through 1994, and this has fueled stock market rallies.

Chile's Stock Market

Stocks trade on the Bolsa de Comercio, in Santiago. The forty-share IPSA index was up 72 percent in 1993. In addition to strong economic growth, corporate profits have continued to be strong, and most state-controlled companies have been privatized. Just as important, Chile's stable democracy has encouraged foreign institutions to become long-term investors.

Extending Free Trade and Improving Its Markets

Chile is not standing still but is taking measures to ensure continued growth and attract investors. It is lowering trade barriers with its neighbors through regional trade pacts and cooperating to improve the functioning of its stock market. In 1992, regulators from Chile, the United States, Canada, and other Latin American countries signed an agreement to toughen and unify regulation of stock exchanges in the Americas. Included in the accord were agreements to:

- Increase the reporting requirements for brokers.
- Speed up dissemination of trading information to the public.
- Monitor more closely investment advisers who work with foreign clients.

C H I N A

Buy

INVESTMENT FACTORS

	1993	1994E
Real Economic Growth:	13.0%	12.0%
Inflation:	12.0%	14.0%
Current Account (% of GDP):	-2.0%	-0.5%

OVERVIEW

Political: China implemented significant economic reforms in 1994, intended, for example, to boost private ownership, further liberalize foreign trade, and reign in the financial system.

Economic: China still has a high-growth policy, but it wants to cool the economy somewhat and avoid runaway inflation, which could threaten reforms. Expect robust double-digit economic growth for 1995.

THE WORLD'S FASTEST-GROWING ECONOMY

China is still a communist state, but its economy has been roaring ahead like a capitalist's dream. Between 1987 and 1991, China's economy grew 8 percent each year, the same stellar pace turned in by other Asian countries, such as Thailand and Taiwan, which are much smaller.

What makes this an Olympic feat is the gargantuan size of China's population (1.2 billion), which makes the chance of its having the world's fastest-growing economy about as likely as an Exxon oil tanker beating a pack of high-speed powerboats in an offshore race. Many economists characterized China's 1992 gains as a one-time "growth spurt," but China whizzed ahead in 1993 to register another 13 percent gain, a trend which continued in 1994.

Consider just how fast China is growing:

- Japan's economy averaged 5 percent growth in the 1970s and 1980s. The Chinese are nearly tripling that growth rate, with ten times Japan's population.
- China is growing two to four times faster than newly industrialized countries outside southeast Asia; from 1988 through 1992, for instance, India grew 5.5 percent annually, Venezuela 4.3 percent and Mexico 3.1 percent.

HOW DID IT HAPPEN?

The economic miracle began when Deng Xiaoping came to power in 1978 and refocused China's priorities on economic growth. He set up economic zones that offered special incentives to companies that produced goods for export. The Chinese entrepreneurial spirit kicked in, and soon foreign companies were shifting their manufacturing capacity to China from the relatively high-wage countries of Taiwan, Korea, and Japan. Chinese exports surged ahead 20 percent, and spawned a kind of "zone fever" as other provinces sought and gained permission to open their own special economic zones. In fact, market reforms have spread like a brushfire across China because of the grassroots success of these regional economic experiments—quite distinct from the experience in post-communist Russia, where economic reforms, imposed from the top down, have not taken hold.

A CHINA INVESTMENT STRATEGY

The best bet is to invest in China through a mutual fund that specializes in the China region (see list). It would be prudent for investors to take advantage of a mutual fund's diversified holdings throughout the China region, rather than leap solely into China's embryonic equities markets. The mutual funds can own B-shares, which trade on China's exchanges, and the H-shares of Chinese companies listed on the Hong Kong Stock Exchange. The funds can also invest in companies in Hong Kong, Taiwan, and the surrounding lesser-developed countries whose economies are increasingly linked with China's and benefit from its growth.

Indeed, a regional approach to investing in China dovetails with the World Bank's view of China, Taiwan, and Hong Kong as "a fourth growth pole" in the global economy, separate from Japan, Europe, and North America.

CHINA FUNDS

Here are eight regional mutual funds that keep a considerable portions of their assets in China and Hong Kong:

CLOSED-END FUNDS ON THE NYSE

	Price (Sept. 1994)	Premium	3-Year	1-Year	% of Assets in China and Hong Kong
Asia Pacific (APB)	$19	19.5%	53%	123%	38
China (CHN)	$19	40.0%	N/A	124%	72
Greater China (GCH)	$19	12.4%	N/A	121%	92
Jardine Fleming China (JFC)	$17	11.1%	N/A	100%	75
Scudder New Asia (SAF)	$25	N/A	36%	95%	23

OPEN-END FUNDS

		Premium	3-Year	1-Year
Merrill Lynch Dragon	(4% load)	28.16%	68.96%	35%
Scudder Pacific Opportunities (NL)		N/A	60.08%	27%
T. Rowe Price New Asia (NL)		33.37%	78.76%	27%

Data from Morningstar.

THE LARGEST MARKET IN THE WORLD

China's expanding economy is putting more money in the pockets of one-quarter of the world's consumers—*its citizens*. From 1978 to 1994, their average income tripled, lifting more than 60 million people out of poverty and into the middle-class (which by the year 2000 is expected to number over 200 million Chinese).

From washing machines to color television sets, Chinese consumers are buying as never before, with the result that Chinese companies are building manufacturing plants at a record clip; imports of industrial equipment have surged, and the Chinese government is encouraging investment in infrastructure, particularly for projects in power generation, transportation, and telecommunications.

As Chinese incomes rise, companies everywhere want to sell those 1.2 billion Chinese a can of diet soda, a pair of designer jeans, and a pack of chewing gum. In 1993, foreign corporations decided to invest $30 billion in China, 30 percent more than they had in 1992. Following are a few recent developments at U.S. companies expanding into China.

- **Procter & Gamble** (NYSE: PG) established three joint ventures: two in laundry detergents, the other in bar soap. These are in addition to the health and beauty-care business P&G began there in 1988. "We continue to see excellent profit potential in China," said John E. Pepper, president of P&G.
- **Anheuser-Busch** (NYSE: BUD) bought a 5 percent stake in China's Tsingtao Brewery Co., which makes the only national brand in China. The country's beer market is growing rapidly; according to the Chinese government, from 1983 to 1993, beer output increased ten-fold.
- **Wrigley** (NYSE: WWY) prices its gum in China at the equivalent of 25 cents a pack, and still its new plant in the Guangdong province cannot keep up with demand.
- **Citibank** (NYSE: CCI) will relocate its area headquarters to Shanghai, from Hong Kong, where as of late 1994, it employed 2,300 people. The bank already has branches or representative offices in several cities along China's coast.

CHINA'S STOCK MARKETS

As recently as 1988, stock exchanges were politically incorrect symbols of capitalism. Now China has two of them: the Shanghai Securities Exchange, established in December 1990, and the Shenzhen Securities Exchange (across from Hong Kong on the mainland), established in April 1991.

Foreign investors look at China's economic future the way World War II soldiers gazed at pinups of Jane Russell. The problem is, it is tough to invest directly in Chinese stocks. Fewer than forty Chinese companies were allowed to sell a special class of stock, called "B" shares, available only to foreign investors. Shares of some Chinese companies are listed on the Hong Kong Stock Exchange (they are called "H" shares) and fall under Hong Kong's regulatory agency.

POLITICS ARE STILL IMPORTANT

Despite the economy's expansion, the Chinese government still has considerable involvement in its direction. Deng Xiaoping, China's current leader and author of its economic reforms, is eighty-nine years old, and rumors of his death have, in the past, sent Chinese share prices tumbling. The concern is that, after his death, his successors might denounce his economic principles. It is unlikely that Chinese officials would risk the outstanding economic gains the country has accrued, but it is important to know why such an event might occur.

China has a deep distrust of foreigners that arose from two contrary experiences in its history. On the one hand, until the nineteenth century China had the confidence of a conqueror, used to receiving tribute from Vietnam, Korea, and, for a time, even Japan. China was the source of culture for the region; its pictorial alphabet, for instance, formed the basis of its neighbors' written languages. On the other hand, China's confidence was shattered when it lost the opium wars of 1839–42 and 1856–60, and Western countries forced trade on it. Japan took Taiwan as booty from the war of 1894-95, and its subsequent twentieth-century colonization of Manchuria was a foreign humiliation China has not forgotten.

1

Ying Xiao is a native Chinese economics professor and author of *China Newsletter*, which educates readers about the investment climate in China. It includes analysis from his trips to China, and his rendering of the current mood of China's central government as it relates to the economy there.

Tell him we sent you and he will send you a complimentary copy of his *China Newsletter*. Regular issues are sent monthly, and an annual subscription is $45.00.

Phone: (909) 247-7810; fax: (909)243-5813;

Address: Aimpacific Associates, 23829 Blue Bill Court, Moreno Valley, CA 92557.

OTHER INVESTMENT RISK FACTORS

Economic change has come so rapidly to China that inflation is rising and could lead to a classic overheated economy, causing at least a pause, if not a bust, in China's economic bubble. The danger to investors would be a precipitous decline in the share prices of Chinese companies.

NET RESULT: BUY, HOLD, AND ADD, TO CHINA REGION INVESTMENTS

There is little possibility that China will revert to its isolationist past. China is a superpower, a permanent member of the U.N. Security Council, and will increasingly help shape solutions to the region's problems; and it has the world's largest consumer market. The chances are that China's rising living standards and economic reforms will prove a potent inducement for investment profits there.

FRANCE

Hold

INVESTMENT FACTORS

	1993	1994E
Real Economic Growth:	-1.0%	2.0%
Inflation:	2.0%	2.0%
Current Account (% of GDP):	1.0%	0.5%
3-month French franc deposits:	8.5%	5.0%
10-year bond yields:	7.0%	7.0%

Political: The government quickly backed down on its initiative to streamline Air France, which brings into question how far the government will go to turn around unprofitable state-owned companies before selling them to private investors in 1994–95.

STOCK MARKET OUTLOOK

France is out of recession, and will experience moderate growth in 1995. French interest rates will likely trend lower and help support stock market growth in 1994-1995. Consider, though, that from 1989 to 1993, the ratio of French stock prices to their earnings (their P/E ratio) doubled to twenty-four.

STOCKS TO CONSIDER

- **Alcatel Alsthom** (NYSE: ALA) This world leader in country telecommunications, energy, and transportation is stepping up its business in Asia, building a power station in China, and winning contracts worth $2.4 billion to build a bullet train in Korea.
- **Elf Acquitaine Group** (NYSE: ELF) The biggest French company is the third largest integrated oil company in Europe and pays a 4.7 percent dividend. By 1996 the French government will have sold most of its 51 percent stake, which should lead to streamlining and improved profitability.
- **Rhone-Poulenc Group** (NYSE: RP) France's largest pharmaceutical company manufactures both prescription drugs and such well-known over-the-counter brands as Maalox. Its dividend yield is 3.0 percent.

- **Valeo** (OTC: VLEOY) One of the world's top auto supply companies, Valeo profited during the severe European downturn and is revved up for 1994's recovery. It received GM's supplier-of-the-year award in 1992. The company is well positioned to take advantage of the upcoming restructuring of Europe's auto industry.

A Closed-end Fund
- **France Growth** (NYSE: FRF) posted consistently solid returns.

Open-end Regional Funds that Invest in France

	1-Year	3-Year	Total Returns % in France
• **Fidelity Europe**	27.16%	6.7%	14
• **Invesco European**	25.88%	5.6%	17
• **PaineWebber Europe Growth**	32.61%	4.8%	18
• **Vanguard Int'l Equity Index - Europe**	29.13%	9.8%	14

Overview

A Modern Financial Services Sector

In the mid-1980s, in preparation for closer economic ties with its European neighbors, France made a commitment to modernize its financial markets, and in the process it has become an attractive destination for the global investor. French shares trade on "la Bourse," the Paris Stock Exchange, the fifth largest in the world. The CAC-40 Index is the most closely watched barometer of the exchange's performance. It used to be that the French placed their savings either in gold or in Paris real estate (the latter soared 15 percent each year through the 1970s and early 1980s). Now they buy stocks, too, and international investors are joining them.

CURRENCY OUTLOOK

The French economy is in good shape, but as part of the European Monetary System, the franc might weaken 10 to 15 percent against the U.S. dollar, along with the D-mark.

A DIVERSIFIED MODERN ECONOMY

France has the world's fourth-largest economy (after the United States, Japan, and Germany). It is the largest country in western Europe and has a highly developed industrial sector and an abundant agricultural potential; three-quarters of France is cultivated farmland. Applying modern technology and government subsidies has made France into Europe's leading agricultural producer (which is why French farmers are a strong political lobby). On the other end of the spectrum, France is a leader in the burgeoning field of financial futures and options, which, in Paris, are traded on the Marche a Terme International de France (MATIF), the fourth-largest futures exchange in the world.

PRIVATIZATIONS WILL BRING TOP FRENCH COMPANIES TO MARKET

The number of companies listed on the Paris Bourse is set to expand dramatically, thanks to the ambitious program to privatize some of the country's best-known companies, announced in 1993 by the new right-wing government. Almost every state-owned company in the competitive sector will go on the block; companies such as Banque Nationale de Paris, Rhone-Poulenc, Air France, and the auto maker Renault are expected to bring at least 300 billion francs ($55 billion) to the government. A previous rule limiting any issue's foreign ownership to 20 percent of the total has been lifted.

2

FRANCE IS SELLING ITS BIG COMPANIES

The French stock market is ready for a record number of share offerings from the privatization of state-controlled industries.

Twenty-one companies across eleven industries are being offered.

Industry	Company
Aerospace:	**Aerospatiale**
	Snecma
Auto:	**Renault**
Banking:	**Banque Nationale de Paris**
	Credit Lyonnais
	Banque Hervet
	Societe Marseillaise de Credit
Chemicals:	**Rhone-Poulenc**
Electronics:	**Groupe Bull**
	Thomson
Insurance:	**AGF**
	Caisse Centrale de Reassurances
	Caisse Nationale de Prevoyance
	GAN
	UAP
Oil:	**Elf-Aquitaine**
Packaging:	**Pechiney**
Steel:	**Usinor-Sacilor**
Tobacco:	**Seita**
Transportation:	**Air France**
	Compagnie Generale Maritime

GERMANY

Hold

INVESTMENT FACTORS

	1993	1994E
Real Economic Growth:	-2.0%	2.0%
Inflation:	3.5%	3.0%
Current Account (% of GDP):	-1.2%	-0.5%
3-month D-mark deposits:	7.0%	5.0%
10-year bond yields:	6.5%	6.7%

Political: Chancellor Helmut Kohl is unpopular and may lose a national election to the Social Democrats, who in previous administrations voted in the generous social programs that Kohl is trying to cut.

STOCK MARKET OUTLOOK

Though the economy was in sharp decline during 1993, lower German interest rates sent the DAX Index to a record high year-end close of 2267, up 36 percent in U.S. dollars. Economic growth is expected, essentially, to pick up slightly in 1995, causing interest rates to fall further, which will encourage the market to register additional gains.

STOCKS TO CONSIDER

- **Deutsche Bank** (NASDAQ: DBKAY) The largest German bank is a major player in Europe. Profits are likely to increase as Europe does better and as German interest rates move lower.
- **Dresdner Bank** (NASDAQ: DRSDY) One of the top ten banks in Europe, Dresdner exemplifies the "universal German bank," providing retail, wholesale, and investment banking services.
- **Daimler Benz** (NYSE: DAI) Germany's largest industrial company, known for its top-quality cars, now trades on the NYSE. Severe cost-cutting and the beginnings of a European

recovery will provide a basis for this stock to be a winner. Buy on weakness.

FOUR CLOSED-END GERMAN FUNDS ON THE NYSE

- **Emerging Germany** (FRG) Favors German stocks likely to benefit from developments in former East Germany and Eastern Europe.
- **Future Germany** (FGF) Particular emphasis on German stocks benefiting from developments in former East Germany.
- **Germany** (GER) Invests in German stocks, and up to 35 percent of its assets in German debt securities.
- **New Germany** (GF) Invests 65 percent of its assets in small- to medium-sized German companies.

OVERVIEW

Germany has the leading economy in Europe. It supplies 35 percent of the economic output of the twelve-nation European Community and its currency, the Deutschemark, is the linchpin of the European monetary system. Like Japan, though, Germany is not self-sufficient in food or raw materials. It pays for the imports it needs by producing sophisticated manufactured goods, chemicals, and complex machine tools for export. An expanding world economy benefits Germany more than most countries.

- Exports represent 25 percent of Germany's economic output, compared with 14 percent for Japan and 8 percent for the United States.

BOND MARKET OUTLOOK

German bonds will continue to be profitable investments because the economic recovery in Germany will be of the stop-and-go variety seen in the United States. Consider a fund that invests solely in German government debt obligations, which are rated AAA/Aaa:

• The Franklin German Government Bond Fund: (800) 342-5236

CURRENCY OUTLOOK

The United States is well into its recovery, whereas Germany is just beginning to improve, and this growth differential will favor the U.S. dollar. The D-mark will probably weaken by 10 to 15 percent against the U.S. currency in the second half of 1994 as U.S. interest rates increase while German rates fall, making the U.S. dollar more attractive to currency investors.

GERMAN STOCKS

From Bayer aspirin to Braun coffee makers and Volkswagen Beetles, many German products have become American household names. More than 80 percent of equity trading in companies that make those and other German products occurs on the Frankfurt Stock Exchange, whose DAX Index is the major barometer of overall German share performance. Similar to our Dow Jones Industrial Average, the DAX Index includes thirty blue-chip stocks. The stocks in the DAX Index account for more than half the total value of all stocks in Germany.

In the fall of 1993, Germany's largest industrial company, **Daimler Benz** (the maker of Mercedes Benz cars), became the first German company to be listed on the New York Stock Exchange (stock symbol: DAI). Other German companies may follow. Meanwhile, four closed-end funds that specialize in Germany also trade on the New York Stock Exchange, in dollars. Mutual funds that specialize in Europe often have 20 percent or more of their assets in Germany.

THE DEUTSCHEMARK IS A STRONG CURRENCY

The Bundesbank (Germany's central bank) is widely viewed as among the most ardent inflation fighters of any central bank in the world. The Bundesbank's harsh anti-inflation polices will keep the German mark a powerful, relatively stable, and, over time, profitable currency to invest in. One way to do so is to buy shares in a mutual fund that invests exclusively in German government bonds, which carry the highest rating of credit quality from Moody's (Aaa) and Standard & Poor's (AAA).

GERMANY WILL BENEFIT FROM THE RECONSTRUCTION OF EASTERN EUROPE

The future of Germany's reunited economy is tied as much to opportunities with the formerly communist countries to its east as it is with its trading partners in the west. As the economic powerhouse of central Europe, Germany will be a major exporter of capital goods to eastern Europe and will take advantage of eastern Europe's more cheaply priced imports and labor rates. But reunification is a long-term investment; *it will not pay quick dividends*. Despite close historical ties and Bonn's deep financial pockets, the $100 billion annual costs of incorporating East Germany have strained the nation and caused soaring federal deficits. (In retrospect, former Bundesbank chief Helmut Schlesinger admits the union was attempted on too ambitious a timetable.)

ON TRACK FOR MODEST GROWTH AND STRUCTURAL CHANGE

The DAX Index reached record highs in late 1993 in anticipation of Germany's emerging from its worst recession since 1949. But Germany's number-one problem is regaining competitiveness; workers in the western part of Germany receive the highest wages and the longest paid vacations in the world, while working the shortest hours compared with workers in other G-7 countries. Though not used to downsizing, German industry is tackling the problem forcefully—three-quarters of eighty companies surveyed expected to reduce their payrolls in 1994–95, and that will put a damper on German growth.

HONG KONG

Buy

INVESTMENT FACTORS

	1993	1994E
Real Economic Growth:	5.5%	5.0%
Inflation:	9.5%	8.0%
Current Account (% of GDP):	2.0%	7.0%

Political: **T minus three years and counting.** . . . Even the 1993 shouting match between Hong Kong and Beijing over democratic reform was considered a "sideshow" compared with the main event driving stock prices: the increasing profits of Hong Kong and Chinese companies.

STOCK MARKET OUTLOOK

Higher, but let's get some perspective. . . . In deference to the largely unquantifiable risks surrounding the colony's 1997 transfer to China, Hong Kong stocks used to trade at twelve to thirteen times earnings while neighboring southeast Asian markets traded at P/Es of 20. The Hang Seng Index, the most-watched barometer of Hong Kong's market, began 1993 at 5,512. In October the index topped 8,000 for the first time, and *Barron's* columnist Peter Du Bois noted that, if Hong Kong P/Es reached 20, the Hang Seng might reach 12,000 a year later—a wildly bullish thought at the time. But the Hang Seng broke 12,000 just two months later, and finished the year at 11,888, up 116 percent.

The Hang Seng—14,000 in 1995: This market experiences notorious downdrafts. Buy a 20 percent to 30 percent correction and buckle your seatbelt. Expect large investors to want to buy in. This should send the market higher, at which time it would be prudent to (1) take profits and (2) wait, again, for the next downdraft, then (3) buy back in.

STOCKS TO CONSIDER
- **China Light and Power** (OTC: CHLWY) Has a proven track record of building power plants and supplying electricity to China.

- **Hong Kong Shanghai Banking Corp.** (OTC: HKSBY) Hong Kong's largest bank has a global empire that is enormously profitable. Group profits were $1.85 billion in 1992, expected at $2.5 billion in 1993, and are predicted to reach $3 billion in 1994, *more money than any bank has ever made.*
- **Hong Kong Telecommunications** (NYSE: HKT) Exclusive local and long-distance provider in Hong Kong. Has had 20 percent growth for the past five years, and double-digit growth is expected to continue. Buy only on dips, though, as the stock has had a phenomenal run.
- **Hopewell Holdings** (OTC: HOWWY) This giant construction, engineering and property developer has $13 billion worth of projects in China.
- **Wharf Holdings** (OTC: WARFY) One of the ten largest Hong Kong companies, it has businesses, from airlines to industrial properties, that are deriving an increasing share of their earnings from China.

NYSE CLOSED-END FUNDS THAT INVEST IN HONG KONG AND CHINA

	Price	Premium	ANNUAL RETURNS 12/31/93		% of Assets in China & Hong Kong
			3-year	1-year	
China (CHN)	$28-1/4	40.0%	N/A	124%	72
Greater China (GCH)	$26-3/4	12.4%	N/A	121%	92
Jardine Fleming China (JFC)	$26	11.1%	N/A	100%	75

OVERVIEW

On July 1, 1997, after being leased for ninety-nine years to Great Britain, Hong Kong will revert back to Chinese control. Although Beijing has considered the 415-square-mile foreign colony on its southern coast to be a historical embarrassment, Hong Kong has also been an economic bonanza for China; up to 40 percent of China's annual foreign currency earnings have been derived from trade and commercial transactions with Hong Kong. The relationship benefits both: Hong Kong has become the primary commercial center financing the economic development of China, and China has become the manufacturing base for Hong Kong businesses (wages in China average one-sixth those in Hong Kong). Hong Kong and China are each other's largest trading partner; total trade between them surpassed $80 billion in 1993. Both economies are booming, and, judging by their investments in each other, Hong Kong and China envision a profitable future together.

- Since 1983, China has substantially increased its holdings in Hong Kong and is the largest foreign investor there, with Hong Kong investments exceeding U.S. $12 billion.
- Hong Kong is the leading investor in China, accounting for nearly two-thirds of the total foreign holdings there. According to a recent Credit Lyonnais survey, companies residing in Hong Kong were involved in 801 projects in China worth at least $67 billion.

THE HONG KONG STOCK EXCHANGE: A STAR PERFORMER

Because so many Hong Kong companies do business in China and have manufacturing operations there, the colony's stock market is considered the leading investment route to China's rapidly growing economy. Hong Kong's links to China sent the Hang Seng Index soaring 116 percent on the Stock Exchange of Hong Kong in 1993.

A GATEWAY TO INVESTMENTS IN CHINA

The Stock Exchange of Hong Kong also lists companies that are owned by the People's Republic of China. The **Bank of China Group**, for example, is the second-largest banking company in Hong Kong. An influx of mainland Chinese businesses are seeking approval to list their shares in Hong Kong and will help vault the Hong Kong stock market into the world's top five, in terms of total share value, by 1997.

POLITICAL RISK VERSUS ECONOMIC OPPORTUNITY

The Hong Kong market is a good long-term investment, but it is also notoriously volatile: Expect a multiyear advance with plenty of sharp corrections. As 1997 approaches, the market, which used to rise and fall whenever Britain and China squabbled over Hong Kong, seems to be developing an immunity to such political scares, but events in China can adversely affect Hong Kong's Hang Seng Index. In 1989, share prices plummeted after pro-democracy students were killed in Beijing's Tiananmen Square.

INDONESIA

Hold

INVESTMENT FACTORS

	1993	1994E
Real Economic Growth:	6.5%	7.0%
Inflation:	10.0%	8.0%
Current Account (% of GDP):	-2.5%	-2.0%

Economy: Expect export growth to continue expanding and domestic spending to increase, which should accelerate economic growth.

STOCK MARKET OUTLOOK

Three to five years out, an investment in Indonesian equities should prove to be a solid winner, but some caution is in order for 1994-1995, especially in view of the Jakarta Stock Exchange's stunning gain of 115 percent in 1993. On the plus side for continued investor profit is the country's economics; Indonesia will continue to be an excellent staging ground for exports, and its domestic economy is growing dramatically. The question of political succession, however ("Who will succeed Suharto?"), will be a persistent "on the back burner" negative and should keep foreign investors from being as bullish on Indonesian stocks as on investments elsewhere in Asia.

STOCK TO CONSIDER
- **Astra International** (OTC: ASINY) This is a diversified holding company that specializes in the automotive industry, which is expanding briskly. Astra is a proxy for the Indonesian economy and should profit accordingly.

CLOSED-END INDONESIAN FUNDS
- **Indonesia Fund** (NYSE: IF) Focuses on Indonesian equities but can also invest in other emerging markets. Up 131 percent in 1993.
- **Jakarta Growth** (NYSE: JGF) Invests in Indonesian equities or fixed-income securities. Up 94 percent in 1993.

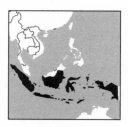

OVERVIEW

OBSCURE GIANT

Question: What is so unusual about a nation of 184 million people (the world's fourth most populous after China, India, and the United States) who reside on 13,000 islands stretching across 3,200 miles?

Answer: It has 350 different ethnic groups, most with their own language, and an economy that's roaring ahead strongly, even by southeast Asia's standards.

Indonesian electrical output is up 1,800 percent from fifteen years ago, and there are twice as many paved roads, but power shortages are still endemic, and Jakarta's traffic jams have become legendary. The government of President Suharto is notorious for human-rights abuses, but its economic policies have brought an improved standard of living to millions. Indonesia's economy has grown by an average of 7 percent a year since Suharto came to power in 1965. Between 1985 and 1993, average incomes tripled for Indonesia's 184 million people and the upward trend is expected to continue through 1995. By 2003, it seems likely, they will double again, by which time the World Bank predicts the that country will have transformed itself into a middle-income nation—not a minor feat.

THE STOCK MARKET

The value of all the shares listed on the Jakarta Stock Exchange was $250 million in 1988; by June 1993, it was $17 billion. In 1993, the market leapt ahead 115 percent but, not surprisingly, in 1994 gave back some of its gains.

THE FUTURE: STRONG GROWTH AMIDST POLITICAL UNCERTAINTY

Although Indonesia's growth potential is enormous, investors worry about who will lead the country after President Suharto; he is seventy-two years old and serving his sixth five-year term. The concern is that, after Suharto's reign, Indonesia, with its scores of islands and ethnic groups, could disintegrate, becoming an Asian Yugoslavia. Such a risk, however, seems far off, and in the meantime Indonesia is prospering rapidly. Indeed, a diversified economic base, vast natural resources, and cheap labor are converting this nation into Asia's newest industrialized country.

ITALY

Stay Away

INVESTMENT FACTORS

	1993	1994E
Real Economic Growth:	-0.5%	2.0%
Inflation:	4.0%	4.0%
Current Account (% of GDP):	0.2%	2.0%
3-month Lire deposits:	10.0%	8.0%
10-year bond yields:	11.0%	10.0%

Political: International confidence has eroded as political uncertainty has increased. After two years of political scandal, Italians elected extremist parties of both the left and right in local elections in November 1993. The 1994 national elections produced a resounding right wing victory.

STOCK MARKET OUTLOOK

Lower Italian interest rates and a sense that Europe was coming out of recession helped Italian stocks increase 48 percent in 1993, though a falling lire lowered that gain, in U.S. dollars, to 28 percent. This market should be considered more risky than other European bourses (stockmarkets) because Italy's economic situation remains shaky. Political chaos has hampered growth and brought to light the problems at state-run companies. Eliminating subsidies to them and restructuring these inefficient giants will be a plus, but such reform will take years to show results.

STOCK TO CONSIDER

- **Montedison** (NYSE: MNT) This leading diversified chemical and agriculture industrial company restructured it bank debt in late 1993, and in many ways mirrors the state of the country at large. This is speculative buy on a company that is restructuring in a country that is recovering.

A CLOSED-END ITALIAN FUND

- **Italy** (NYSE: ITL) For the venturesome investor, this fund is a diversified play on Italy's stock market. Up 38 percent in 1993, with solid 1994–95 performance expected.

OVERVIEW

Sometimes it is less risky to invest in a market that has taken its lumps and is recovering. Italy fits that bill. From 1987 through 1992, the Italian stock market was pulled down 50 percent by an inefficient state-owned industrial sector that controlled more than half the nation's economic output. Then, just when other European markets were picking up, Italy was wracked by a widening corruption scandal in which more than 2,500 politicians and businessmen were implicated in passing bribes and illegal donations for public-works contracts. If the scandal, eventually called "Tangentopoli," or "bribe city," has a silver lining, it is that Italian voters finally had enough. In 1993, they swept incumbent politicians out of office, no matter what their party.

THE MARKET APPLAUDED

Italy has ten separate stock markets, but more than 90 percent of the trading volume occurs on the Milan Stock Exchange. Milan's market was enthusiastic over the prospect of wide-ranging economic and political reforms, gaining over 35 percent in 1993, almost twice the increases registered by France and the U.K. If Italy follows through with implementing reforms, its economic growth will likely outpace the rest of Europe's during the second half of the decade, and its stock market will continue to be a frontrunner.

CURRENCY OUTLOOK

European currencies in general will weaken against the U.S. dollar in late 1994 due to higher growth in the United States. The Italian lire will likely follow, declining 10 percent to 15 percent in 1994–95.

THE NEW DEVELOPMENTS

- Eight out of ten Italians voted in April 1993 to change the electoral system. In early 1994, Parliament passed an electoral-reform bill.
- The new reform government came up with a budget that will begin to curb the growth of Italy's vast public debt, which has grown to more than 100 percent of Gross Domestic Product.
- The prime minister confronted government unions, which represent 3.5 million employees, and negotiated a groundbreaking agreement to improve the productivity and quality of public services.

ITALY'S PRIVATIZATIONS TO BOOST PRODUCTIVITY

Italy has an ambitious schedule of privatizations that could raise more than $50 billion through 1998 to help cut its horrendous budget deficit. The boot-shaped country has always had two distinct economies—one private, the other government controlled—and if the privatized companies take after their industrious, productive private-sector cousins, they should improve markedly. Consider that with its corrupt, inefficient state-controlled industries, Italy's private sector still powered the country's overall economy to a 2 percent annual growth rate during the 1980s.

PRIVATIZATIONS WILL BE A PLUS FOR THE MARKET

Italy expects to sell up to 75 percent of the privatized stock in overseas markets, but if the new issues do not trade well at home, they will not sell well abroad. So, the government has devised incentives for Italian investors to help make those stocks popular in Italy. This will help attract foreign institutional investors to the new issues, which will dramatically increase Milan's trading volume. The result will be bullish for this reconstituted market.

JAPAN

Hold

INVESTMENT FACTORS

	1993	1994E
Real Economic Growth:	-0.5%	1.0%
Inflation:	1.2%	0.5%
Current Account (% of GDP):	3.0%	2.5%
3-month Yen deposits:	3.0%	2.0%
10-year bond yields:	4.2%	4.0%

Political: Japan's prime minister resigned. The diverse seven-party ruling coalition split up. With a depressed economy and the dogged Liberal Democratic Party back in power, with the Socialists, expect a call for new elections by the middle of 1995.

STOCK MARKET OUTLOOK

Japan's ailing economy will see some relief in 1995; output will be slightly higher than 1994, but a second dip into recession is a possibility. Record low interest rates, by themselves, will not do the trick, and Japan's bureaucrats, unfortunately, have blocked substantive measures to stimulate the economy. Unless the dollar rallies, the Nikkei 225 Index may decline and stay below 20,000 in 1995.

CLOSED-END JAPANESE FUNDS ON THE NYSE

	Total Returns 1993
• **Japan Equity** (JEQ)	86.6%
• **Japan OTC Equity** (JOF)	29.5%

Overview

By any calculation, Japan's postwar rise to productive preeminence has verged on the miraculous. A strong work ethic, comparatively small defense expenditures, and an unusual brand of capitalism based on mutual cooperation between government and industry has helped Japan develop one of the most sophisticated economies in the world. Japanese GDP averaged a 10 percent annual surge in the 1960s and, despite oil shocks and a rising yen, the economy averaged 5 percent growth in the 1970s and 1980s. It is all the more noteworthy that Japan, a country slightly smaller than California, achieved this with negligible mineral resources of its own.

The Japanese Stock Market

The Tokyo Stock Exchange is Japan's primary equity market; its Nikkei 225 Stock Index has tracked Japan's advance from a production-based economy that relied on imported technology to one with numerous companies on the technological cutting edge of their industries. In July 1965, the Nikkei was 1,020. In October 1982 it was 6,850; then a combination of declining interest rates, plummeting oil prices, and a skyrocketing yen contributed to the Nikkei's soaring almost 600 percent, by the end of 1989, to 38,915. Though Japan's stock market is currently the world's second largest (behind that of the United States), at one point in 1988 the combined market value of Japanese stocks was almost 1-1/2 times greater than the total value of U.S. stocks.

1989: A Reality Check for Japanese P/E Ratios

By 1989, the price-to-earnings ratio of Japanese stocks had skyrocketed to over 80, more than three times their average during the 1970s and early 1980s, and four times the P/E ratio of U.S. stocks. In

1990, Japan's rapidly growing economy pushed bond interest rates up to 8 percent, and the speculative bubble burst. In nine months, the Nikkei Index had fallen back to levels of four years earlier.

CURRENCY OUTLOOK

Weak economic performance will not sustain an overvalued yen, which will trend lower. The U.S. dollar will likely strengthen. By 1996, it may take 120 to 130 yen to buy one dollar, up from 100 in the fall of 1994.

STOCK MARKET STRATEGY

Wait for the yen to weaken and more bearish news on the Japanese economy to come out, then invest in a mutual fund specializing in Japan or an Asian fund with a significant investment exposure in Japan. In this difficult environment it is essential to have the risk diversification that a fund offers.

THE JAPANESE ECONOMY IS RESILIENT

From surges in oil prices to a rising yen, the island nation has been dealt so many economic shocks that the Japanese have coined a nickname for them: "Tsunamis," the word for the tidal waves that, throughout Japan's history, have arrived suddenly and devastated coastal areas. Japanese companies have survived economic Tsunamis before through cost-cutting and innovation, with a focus on product quality. But to continue to stay competitive Japan is having to build and operate plants abroad—and not just to avoid protectionism caused by its huge trade surpluses. The low-wage centers in Asia are China, Korea, Malaysia, and other neighboring countries; Japan no longer is such a center. Japanese factory workers now earn, on average, the same wages as U.S. workers. In 1994, Japan imported more televisions than it exported; the TVs came from Japanese-owned factories in southeast Asia. This trend will continue. Japan will provide capital, equipment, and expertise to its overseas factories, which in turn will provide it with products and profits.

A SOARING YEN AND JAPAN'S TRADE SURPLUS

The yen almost reached 100 to the dollar in 1993. At that level the Nikkei Index was worth more in dollars than at its peak in 1989. The prospect of the yen's rising further was seen threatening Japan's economic growth, so the Prime Minister made pledges to stimulate Japan's economy and open the country to more imports. In response, the U.S. Federal Reserve intervened in global currency markets and halted a further rise in the yen's value.

Almost half of the United States' entire deficit is with Japan, and a lower dollar has not helped to curb it. This is why the United States has pressured Japan to make the structural reforms that are necessary to open its economy to more imports. For example, Japan has thousands of import restrictions; two out of five date back to the 1950s and 1960s, when Japan was an economic small-fry. Japanese consumers will benefit along with American exporters if their government loosens its vise-like regulation of imports; American apples brought into Japan are expected to sell for 50 cents each rather than the $5.00 price tag commanded by the home-grown brand's monopoly.

If Japan shows substantive progress, then the yen will stabilize or decline against the dollar; otherwise the yen will continue its long-term uptrend.

WAYS TO INVEST

There are many ways to profit from economic growth in Japan. Mutual-fund companies have established funds that specialize in Japanese equities, and there are closed-end funds, going back to 1964, when **The Japan Fund, Inc.,** was listed on the New York Stock Exchange. In addition, U.S. brokerage firms have expanded their research coverage of Japan, so brokers can recommend promising Japanese stocks, whether Japanese ADRs like **Sony Corporation** (SNE) on the New York Stock Exchange or equities such as **Nintendo Entertainment Co.** on the Tokyo Stock Exchange.

OPEN-ENDED JAPANESE MUTUAL FUNDS

	Average Annual Total Returns to 12/31/93	
	1-Year	3-Year
• **Fidelity Japan**	20.45%	N/A
• **G.T. Japan Growth**	33.45%	3.05%
• **Japan Fund**	23.64%	3.33%

OPEN-END PACIFIC FUNDS

| | Average Annual Total Returns | | % of Assets |
	1-Year	3-Year	in Japan
• **Fidelity Pacific Basin**	63.91%	23.26%	36%
• **GAM Pacific Basin**	51.01%	22.38%	36%
• **Merrill Lynch Pacific A**	34.47%	14.47%	73%

POLITICAL CHANGE

Today the Tsunami that Japan faces is political. After thirty-eight years of one-party rule, the Liberal Democratic Party lost the July 1993 national election. The stench of corruption amongst Japan's iron triangle of big business, bureaucrats, and politicians was too much for voters who overturned the LDP's hammerlock on Japan's Diet, the 511-seat legislative body. But the victory was narrow, and a succession of prime ministers followed. With a sluggish economy and companies like **Honda** and **Nippon Steel** posting losses, the new prime minister will have to spur the economy, or another election will follow.

KOREA

Buy

INVESTMENT FACTORS

	1993	1994E
Real Economic Growth:	5.0%	8.0%
Inflation:	5.0%	8.5%
Current Account (% of GDP):	-1.5%	-0.5%

Political: Because North Korea is bankrupt, its nuclear sabre rattling can be viewed as its last bargaining chip. Unsettling as that might be, given worldwide diplomatic concern, the most likely scenario is actually a lowering of hostilities between the two Koreas.

STOCK MARKET OUTLOOK

Although the Korean Composite Index was up 28 percent in 1993, its gains were less impressive than those of its neighbors because of North Korea's threats and the ongoing restructuring of South Korea's economy. With strong economic growth expected and a lowering of tensions between North and South, the stock market should do better in 1995.

CLOSED-END FUNDS

For those willing to take the risk, the most practical way is to invest in one of the closed-end Korean country funds that trade on the New York Stock Exchange:

	Share Price 9/7/94	Premium to Portfolio Value	1993 Total Return
Korea Fund (NYSE: KF)	$25	42%	+71.5%
Korean Investment Fund (NYSE: KIF)	$15	45%	+69.4%
Korean Equity Fund (NYSE: KEF)	$12	29%	N/A

Do not be worried by fund prices that reflect premiums of up to 40 percent above the value of the stocks in their portfolios. Korean funds typically trade at significant premiums because it is not possible for foreign individuals to buy directly on the Seoul exchange, and the Korean government severely restricts the number of investment funds that can operate, giving the ones that do a monopoly and causing their shares to trade at a premium.

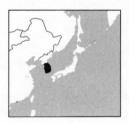

OVERVIEW

From 1970 into 1994, South Korea's economy grew faster than any other in the world. Korean exports of labor-intensive products such as footwear and textiles, as well as automobiles, ships, and steel, propelled it to an average 9 percent annual growth rate.

A RESILIENT AND ADAPTABLE PEOPLE

South Korea's industrial development has taken place in difficult surroundings: on a narrow peninsula off communist China, beneath an armed and menacing North Korea. In fact, the paths taken by South and North Korea provide an object lesson in the benefits of an open versus closed economic system. The Korean War (1950–53) split a population that had a common history and distinct culture; South Korea developed a booming export-oriented economy, while North Korea sought self-sufficiency and became one of the world's most isolated economies. The result: South Korea's 1994 economy was approximately fourteen times larger than North Korea's, which, ironically, after the political separation of Korea, wound up with most of the peninsula's substantial mineral and hydroelectric resources.

THE KOREAN STOCK MARKET

The Korean Stock Exchange (KSE) is located in Seoul, on a large island in the Han River. Though the Korean Composite Stock Price Index was up 28 percent in 1993, the waters have been turbulent thereafter for investors on the KSE. Share prices were volatile, in part, because of the ongoing restructuring of Korea's economy; it finds itself sandwiched between the world's advanced economies and those paying lower wages in southeast Asia and China. In response, Korean businesses have been retooling manufacturing plants to produce more sophisticated goods, but such changes slowed overall economic growth to about 5 percent in 1994.

North Korea destabilized the market in 1994 by rattling its nuclear sabre. Underlying that problem is North Korea's economy; it is on the verge of collapse. To forestall that prospect, Seoul wants increased economic cooperation with Pyongyang, and ultimately reunification with the north. The most likely outcome, *eventually*, is that North Korea will give up its nuclear weapons capability for economic security; meanwhile, its threats cannot be taken lightly— almost one million soldiers still face off against one another along Korea's 150-mile-long demilitarized zone.

THE FUTURE: BULLISH FOR INVESTORS IN KOREA

While South Korea has been living and prospering for decades with a hostile neighbor just above it, North Korea's sabre rattling makes any Korean investment speculative. However, South Korea has proven itself adaptable to changing global circumstances, and its stock market should prove profitable to foreign investors. Economic growth is picking up and reached a 6 percent annual rate during 1994. Korea is taking steps to remove trade barriers, open up its economy, and liberalize foreign investment rules, all of which is bullish for its stock market.

MALAYSIA

Buy

INVESTMENT FACTORS

	1993	1994E
Real Economic Growth:	8.5%	8.5%
Inflation:	3.5%	4.5%
Current Account (% of GDP):	-3.0%	-2.5%

Economic: Expect strong economic growth into 1995, stimulated by demand for Malaysia's exports, a national budget that provides for infrastructure development and increased domestic consumption spurred in part by the increased wealth caused by Malaysia's stock market boom.

STOCK MARKET OUTLOOK

No doubt, when the KLSE Composite Index finished 1993 up 98 percent, 1994 was ripe for a correction. In 1995, buy the dips in this market, though, because the long-term outlook for the Malaysian stock market is good.

STOCKS TO CONSIDER

Just one of Malaysia's blue chips, **Sime Darby**, trades in the United States. Look for the others, particulary Telekom Malaysia, to be listed on the NYSE in the form of American Depositary Receipts.

- **Sime Darby** (OTC: SIDBY) Sime Darby is Malaysia's second-largest company. It has extensive holdings in plantation companies, heavy equipment, and airlines and, with more than 170 subsidiary companies, is involved in just about every aspect of Malaysia's economy. Foreign operations in Hong Kong, Australia, the Philippines, and Singapore accounted for 30 percent of group profits.

A CLOSED-END MALAYSIA FUND

- **Malaysia Fund** (NYSE: MF) Provides a diversified entry to Malaysia's markets. Up 80.2 percent in 1993, with a three-year average annual return of 36.6 percent.

REGIONAL FUNDS THAT INVEST IN MALAYSIA

Malaysia is also a favorite with mutual funds that invest in Asia.

CLOSED-END FUNDS ON THE NYSE

	Price	Premium	ANNUAL RETURNS		% of Assets in Malaysia
			3-year	1-year	
Asia Pacific (APB)	$25-1/2	19.5%	53%	123%	20%
Scudder New Asia (SAF)	$27-3/8	N/A	36%	95%	12%

OPEN-END FUNDS

Merrill Lynch Dragon	(4% load)	28.16%	68.96%	30%
Scudder Pacific Opportunities	(nl)	N/A	60.08%	12%
T. Rowe Price New Asia	(nl)	33.37%	78.76%	28%

Data from Morningstar.

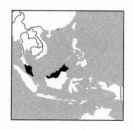

OVERVIEW

Don't tell the Malays their country is going to become one of Asia's economic tigers; they're already convinced it is one. On ninety-five acres in Kuala Lumpur, the political and financial capital of Malaysia, construction has begun on what will be the tallest building in the world, a structure higher than the 110-story Sears Tower in Chicago. Kuala Lumpur also has a new $3 billion airport.

THE EMERGENCE OF A MANUFACTURING HEAVYWEIGHT

Not long ago Malaysia had a farm-based economy, and while its plantation companies are huge, after years of impressive growth it is the country's booming manufacturing sector that is driving economic growth, and drawing outside investment. In July 1993, Chrysler began manufacturing Jeep vehicles in a plant just outside Kuala Lumpur. This is the company's only manufacturing operation in southeast Asia. American corporations have invested a total of $32 billion in Malaysia, and Japan's have invested almost twice that much. Consider the strength and diversity of Malaysia's economy:

- Malaysia's 18 million people are the richest in Asia, after those of Japan and the four Tigers: Hong Kong, Singapore, Taiwan, and South Korea.
- Malaysia is the world's largest exporter of computer chips. (Also, **Motorola Inc.**, a major U.S. chip manufacturer, has four factories there, employing 12,000 people.)
- Malaysia's **Perusahaan Otomobil Nasional Bhd.** is a locally owned car manufacturer—the only one in southeast Asia. Japan's Mitusbishi Motors Corporation is a 17 percent owner of the company. In 1985, 8,400 Proton "Sagas" cars were sold; in 1993, more than 100,000 were sold, and the trend continues.

THE KUALA LUMPUR EXCHANGE

The country's largest companies are in telecommunications, shipping, financial, electrical, and auto manufacturing industries, and they are listed on the Kuala Lumpur Stock Exchange (KLSE). Although it is usually described as an emerging market, owning stocks listed on the KLSE may be one of the best ways to profit from the industrialization of southeast Asia.

CURRENCY OUTLOOK

From 1986 to 1992, the Malaysian ringitt traded at an average price of 38 cents. In 1993, it averaged 39 cents. The ringitt should remain stable against the U.S. dollar in 1995 and, if anything, appreciate slightly toward 39.5 cents to 40 cents.

3
MALAYSIA'S BIGGEST BLUE CHIPS

- Automaker: **Perusahaan Otomobil Nasional Bhd.**
- Conglomerate: **Sime Darby**
- Construction: **UMV Holdings Bhd.**
- Electric utility: **Tenaga Nasional Bhd.**
- Semiconductor maker: **Malaysian Pacific Industries Bhd.**
- Telecommunications: **Telekom Malaysia Bhd.**

MEXICO

Buy

INVESTMENT FACTORS

	1993	1994E
Real Economic Growth:	1.0%	2.5%
Inflation:	8.0%	7.0%
Current Account (% of GDP):	-6.0%	-7.0%

Politics: President Carlos Salinas achieved political and economic reforms culminating in the North American Free Trade Agreement, yet he resorted to severe measures to crush a 1994 New Year's uprising in the southern Mexico. His succesor's challenge will be to strike a balance between firmness to secure social order and a commitment to ongoing reform so as not to scare off foreign investors.

STOCK MARKET OUTLOOK

Mexico's Bolsa (stock market) roared ahead 48 percent in 1993, and the three- to five-year outlook is bullish as NAFTA and economic reforms stimulate growth on two fronts: new factories to manufacture goods for domestic consumption and export, and a new infrastructure to meet the needs of Mexicans with rising disposable incomes.

STOCKS TO CONSIDER

- **Cemex** (OTC: CMXBY) Mexico's largest cement maker should benefit from economic growth and infrastructure projects.
- **Grupo Radio Centro** (NYSE: RC) The country's number-one radio broadcasting system has a fast-growing revenue base and more than 30 percent of Mexico City's radio market.
- **Telefonos de Mexico** (NYSE: TMX) This company has a great franchise. Phone-line growth is running at 13 to 14 percent a year, about three times the U.S. rate; look for it to increase as more Mexicans are able to afford telephones.
- **Transportacion Maritima Mexicana** (NYSE: TMM) The dominant Mexican shipping company will give its U.S. counterparts a run for the money.

- **Vitro, S.A.** (NYSE: VTO) The leading glass maker in Mexico has a growing automotive business. Its products cost less than its U.S. competitors'; with NAFTA, Vitro will likely increase sales to the United States.

Closed-end Mexican Country Funds
- **Mexico Fund** (NYSE: MXF) Invests primarily in Mexican stocks. Began in June 1981 and has three-year, five-year, and ten-year average annual returns of over 40 percent. Up 84 percent in 1993 with continued growing into 1995.
- **Mexico Equity & Income** (NYSE: MXE) Invests up to 80 percent in Mexican equities with the balance in convertibles, cash, or bonds. Began August 1990. Up 87.5 percent in 1993.

A North American Income Fund
Dean Witter markets a mutual fund, the **North American Government Income Trust**, which is run by Trust Company of the West (TC West), which invests up to 25 percent of the fund's assets in Mexican Treasury bills. Up to 10 percent of the fund's assets can be invested in Canadian government bills, with the balance in U.S. government–guaranteed securities. The fund's blended yield was around 7.23 percent throughout 1994.

Overview
With 85 million people and a GDP of 165 billion, Mexico has three times Canada's population and one-third its total economic output. Mexico is the world's sixth-largest producer of oil and natural gas, and it exports over half its production. In the early 1980s, Mexico was too dependent on oil exports; when the price of oil collapsed, Mexico's economy was devastated, along with its credit rating. Since

then the country has strengthened its manufacturing base, and oil is down to 30 percent of GDP. Mexico has a wealth of mineral deposits—it is the world's largest producer of silver—and exports prodigious quantities of fruit, vegetables, grain, and coffee.

EFFECTS OF ECONOMIC REFORM

With the implementation of the North American Free Trade Agreement (NAFTA), Mexico is poised to benefit from economic reforms achieved under Mexican President Salinas.

- Single-digit Inflation. Annual inflation is below 10 percent for the first time in twenty years, and down from triple digits in 1987.

- Lower Taxes and a Budget Surplus. From running a deficit that averaged 12 percent of GDP in the late 1980s, Mexico turned in budget surpluses in 1991, 1992 and 1993, *and* its GDP grew over 2.5 percent annually in the process—all this while corporate and individual tax rates were slashed to 35 percent, from 60.5 percent and 42 percent, respectively. (Note to all Washington D.C. budget pundits: Try that sombrero on for size—please!)

- Higher Per Capita Income. Economic growth is now outpacing population growth, with the average Mexican earning slightly over $4,000 annually, up from $2,000 in 1989. The result is an increase in disposable income for each Mexican worker, which is being spent on more goods and services. This is propelling the Mexican economy forward.

PRIVATIZATIONS HAVE SLICED GOVERNMENT'S SHARE OF GDP IN HALF

The government's share of national spending has been reduced to 25 percent, down from 44.5 percent in 1982. In 1982, the government owned or controlled 1,155 enterprises. By mid-1994, it had sold off 938 businesses, including copper and coal mines, two television networks, **Telefonos de Mexico** (**Telemex**, the national telephone company), and all eighteen of the country's commercial banks. Privatized companies have increased their operating efficiency, and this is reducing the need for government subsidies they previously received.

THE BOLSA

Mexico's stock market, the Bolsa Mexicana de Valores, has grown in sophistication and importance. The primary stock market index is the IPC (Indice de Precios y Cotizaciones). Investors who bought depressed Mexican stocks in 1982 made the big kill if they held on to them until 1992. By then the Bolsa had soared to more than eighty times its 1982 value—adjusted for U.S. dollars! This rise prompted the listing of several Mexican companies on U.S. exchanges, and many more have followed. There are mutual funds that specialize in Latin American and Mexican stocks, and two closed-end Mexican funds on the New York Stock Exchange.

CURRENCY OUTLOOK

With foreign investment pouring in because of NAFTA, the Mexican peso should depreciate by just 3 percent in 1994, well within the official targets.

THE NEW PESO

Mexico allows its exchange rate to fluctuate within a range that allows for pre-programmed mini-devaluations. With a relatively stable exchange rate and real interest rates at close to the highest levels in the world, there has also been another way to profit in Mexico: owning ninety-day Mexican government paper—in pesos. Investors in the Mexican currency profited when Mexican interest rates stayed more than twice as high as the decline in the peso against the dollar. With all the foreign money invested in Mexico, its peso has declined less than expected, but it's important to remember that to achieve dollar profits on a peso investment, a U.S. investor must achieve returns greater than the rate of peso devaluation.

NEW ZEALAND

Buy

INVESTMENT FACTORS

	1993	1994E
Real Economic Growth:	3.0%	4.0%
Inflation:	2.0%	3.0%
3-month NZ$ deposits:	5.5%	5.5%
10-year bond yields:	7.5%	7.5%

Economic: There is an air of optimism in New Zealand. It has emerged from recession with a stronger economy because of improved efficiencies gained from a comprehensive program of economic reform. According to one report, New Zealand ranks first, for long-term competitiveness, among OECD nations (Japan is number two; the United States is number twelve).

STOCK MARKET OUTLOOK

Though the NZSE-40 index was up 40 percent for 1993, expect slightly less impressive gains in 1995. The 1980s saw a sluggish economy and 10 percent unemployment for New Zealand; the hoped-for improvements after economic reforms began to be felt only in 1992 and 1993. After restructuring itself, New Zealand is now well positioned to benefit from increasing growth in the economies of its Asian trading partners.

STOCKS TO CONSIDER:

Given its relatively small size, most Asia/Pacific funds have less than 5 percent of their investments in New Zealand. If you want exposure to New Zealand's market, you may do well to buy these stocks, which account for 25 percent of New Zealand's stock market value.

- **Fletcher Challenge** (NYSE: FLC) This diversified company has interests ranging from the oil and gas business to pulp and paper and building materials, including logs, wood, steel, and cement.
- **Telecom New Zealand** (NYSE: NZT) Telecom is the principal supplier of all telecommunications services in New

Zealand. It has cut costs, is the leading provider of cellular services, and has healthy earnings. It should benefit from increasing investor awareness of New Zealand. Bell Atlantic and Ameritech are part owners. Dividend yield of over 8 percent.

- **Fletcher Forests** (NYSE: FFC) In December 1993, Fletcher Challenge spun off 50 percent of its forests division, which owns pine plantations in New Zealand and Chile. With log prices up, and tree harvesting down in North America and southeast Asia, this is an investment in an asset, radiata pine trees, which, according to chief executive Hugh Fletcher, "could increase in value annually by 8 percent to 9 percent" above inflation. In the fiscal year to June 30, 1993, the company earned (in New Zealand dollars) $108 million on sales of two million cubic meters of logs. We anticipate continued growth in 1995.

OVERVIEW

New Zealand is the most physically isolated of the advanced industrialized countries. Its closest neighbor, Australia, is 1,200 miles away.

This island country, larger than Great Britain, is well positioned to profit from Asia's extraordinary economic growth and rising incomes. Asia needs electric generating capacity; New Zealand has abundant offshore natural gas reserves and more than 3 billion tons of coal reserves that can help fuel Asia's new generators. The country's greatest prospects, though, are in farming.

- New Zealand is the world's largest and most competitive producer of dairy products.
- It is a major exporter of fish, beef, and fresh fruit.
- Sheep outnumber New Zealand's 3.5 million people by 20 to 1 and make the country the world's second-largest wool exporter and the largest exporter of lamb and mutton.

THE STOCK MARKET

Equities trade in Wellington on the New Zealand Stock Exchange (NZSE), and the NZSE 40-Share Index measures its performance. In 1993 the country shook off a long recession and the index rose 40 percent.

KEEPING THE AGRICULTURAL ADVANTAGE

New Zealand did away with most of its farm subsidies in the mid-1980s and in the process has become one of the world's most efficient agricultural exporting nations. The government does fund research that attempts to make New Zealand agriculture more competitive and responsive to changing global markets. For instance, such research has included improving processes for refrigerated transportation, which expanded the reach of New Zealand's farm trade. The goal is to produce and sell specialized farm products, not bulk exports, and deliver them to world markets.

INVESTING IN NEW ZEALAND AGRICULTURE

New Zealand is one of the world's most competitive agricultural exporters. For the venturesome investor, here are six agricultural companies listed on the New Zealand Stock Exchange:

Applefields

Corporate Investments

Fortex

Mainzeal

Mair Astley

Reid Farmers

CURRENCY OUTLOOK

In the 1980s, the New Zealand dollar plunged, demoralizing foreign investors along the way; but in 1993, the "Kiwi dollar" rallied and is now perceived as a relatively strong currency. After the election of the conservative government in 1990, the central bank added to its charter a clause stating that the central bank must protect the foreign value of the New Zealand dollar. Other than Germany's Bundesbank, few central banks place as high a priority on guarding the external value of their country's currency. This should make investing in their stocks even more profitable in 1995–96.

PHILIPPINES

Buy

INVESTMENT FACTORS

	1993	1994E
Real Economic Growth:	2.5%	4.5%
Inflation:	8.0%	10.0%
Current Account:	-6.0%	-7.5%

Politics: Foreign investors and bankers give President Fidel Ramos high marks for bringing political stability to the Philippines, something notably absent prior to his election in 1992.

STOCK MARKET OUTLOOK

After 1993's surge of 154 percent, a time-out in the market's rise was in order. During 1995, buy the market on dips in price, as Manila's market should be a good long-term bet. Overall economic activity in 1995 is expected to grow 3.5 percent, and inflation should decline further. Stick to blue-chip stocks if investing directly in stocks there. Otherwise, a mutual fund that specializes in global emerging markets or an Asian mutual fund should profit by including a portion of its investment assets in the Philippine stock market.

STOCKS TO CONSIDER
- **Benguet Corp.** (NYSE: BE) This gold and chromite producer employs 13,000 personnel, represents 1 percent of the market index, and has been listed on the NYSE since 1949.
- **Philippines Long Distance** (ASE: PHI) A major expansion and modernization program is underway at this company, which supplies 94 percent of telephone service in the Philippines. The stock zoomed up from a low of $35 a share to $85 in 1994, so wait for a pullback and then buy for a long-term play.
- **San Miguel Corp.** (OTC: SMGBY) The largest food and beer producer in the Philippines has a brewery in Hong Kong and China. As of 1994, exports were about 14 percent of sales.

A CLOSED-END PHILIPPINE FUND

- **First Philippine Fund** (NYSE: FPF) This fund invests up to 80% of its assets in Philippine stocks. Up 134.2 percent in 1993.

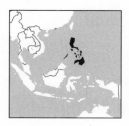

OVERVIEW

Part of the reason the market has done so well is that it was so cheap; the economy had just finished several years of poor growth, aggravated by natural disasters, including the eruption of Mount Pinatubo, which forced the closing of Clark Air Force Base. In 1992, a prolonged drought and severe power outages caused the Philippine economy to shrink by half a percent, while the economies of neighboring countries galloped ahead. Once considered southeast Asia's economic laggard, the Philippine stock market left 1993's other big winners in the dust, even Malaysia (+98 percent) and Hong Kong (+116 percent). With gains of 154 percent, the Manila Stock Exchange was 1993's global star performer. Some of the Philippines' problems continue to be daunting; half of its 65 million people live in poverty, and a large income gap exists between rich and poor.

SO WHY WAS THE STOCK MARKET UP SHARPLY?

Political stability is the key reason why equity portfolio managers believe that Ayala Avenue—Manila's Wall Street—has turned around. Six coup attempts against President Corazon Aquino frightened off investors during the 1980s, even when the economy was growing at an average 4 percent clip. Fidel Ramos won the May 1992 presidential elections to succeed Aquino. Educated in the United States at West Point, Ramos (the former Philippine defense chief) has been praised for his consensus building, which has helped him achieve a list of solid accomplishments. For example, he implemented a fast-track approval process for the creation of new electric generators, which by 1994-1995, are expected to eliminate the power shortages that have dogged manufacturers' ability to produce goods.

OTHER BLUE CHIPS ON THE PHILIPPINE STOCK EXCHANGE

Here are the three top Philippine companies. They are tomorrow's winners and may become listed on U.S. exchanges as American Depository Receipts.

> **Ayala Corporation**: The oldest and largest Philippine conglomerate.
>
> **Globe Telecom**: Operates high-tech telecommunications.
>
> **Philippine National Bank**: The country's largest commercial bank.

OTHER ENCOURAGING SIGNS

- Economic Growth Rates Are Better Than They Appear. Growth for the Philippines, while low for southeast Asia, is in line with Mexico (3.0 percent growth) and other emerging economies.

- Inflation Is Relatively Low. Inflation is running at 8 percent, down from 13 percent in 1991. (The Philippines' average inflation rate from 1983 to 1992 was 15 percent, lower than those of Portugal, Turkey, Argentina, and Mexico—countries that all were given higher credit ratings by Moody's Investor Services and Standard & Poor's Corporation.)

- Foreign Debt Has Been Reduced. The Philippines restructured its foreign bank debt, reducing it by more than $6 billion. Improved tax receipts and privatizations have reduced government borrowings and increased monies available for infrastructure investment.

SINGAPORE

Buy

INVESTMENT FACTORS

	1993	1994E
Real Economic Growth:	8.5%	9.0%
Inflation:	3.0%	3.5%
Current Account (% of GDP):	2.5%	2.0%

Economics: Expect Singapore's strong economic expansion to continue. Besides having a strong economy, virtually no political risk, and good infrastructure, Singapore companies also have extensive business dealings with China. All of this bodes well for Singapore's economic prospects.

STOCK MARKET OUTLOOK

The Straits Times Industrial Index was up 59 percent in 1993. It should continue to be a winner in the next three to five years, not only because of Singapore's strong export growth but also because the country is the leading seller of financial and other services to the expanding economies in the region.

STOCKS TO CONSIDER
- **Development Bank of Singapore** (OTC: DEVBY) This is the largest bank in Singapore, which is the financial center for southeast Asia's dynamic economies.
- **Keppel Corp.** (OTC: KPELY) This diversified holding company's primary business is ship repair and building, but it also has interests in banking, telecommunications, engineering, and real estate.

A CLOSED-END SINGAPORE FUND
- **Singapore Fund** (NYSE: SGF) At least 65 percent of the fund will be invested in Singapore, the balance in other southeast Asian markets. The fund was up a mammoth 154 percent in 1993, but with its year-end price carrying a premium of 31.7 percent, an investor considering Singapore would do better to

wait to buy until the glow is off this market so that the premium and the fund's price are lower.

A CLOSED-END FUND THAT INVESTS IN SINGAPORE

	12/31/93 Price	Premium	Annual Returns 3-year	1-year	% of Assets in Singapore
Asia Pacific (APB)	$25-1/2	19.5%	53%	123%	18
OPEN-END FUNDS WITH INVESTMENTS IN SINGAPORE					
Merrill Lynch Dragon (4% load)			28.16%	68.96%	4
T. Rowe Price New Asia (nl)			33.37%	78.76%	13

Data from Morningstar.

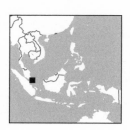

OVERVIEW

Lying just off the southern tip of Malaysia is an independent city-state. Thirteenth-century Sumatran settlers dubbed the area "Singa Pur," Sanskrit for "city of the lion." A presumptuous name then, perhaps, but today it is an apt title for one of Asia's most dynamic economic powerhouses.

THE ECONOMIC CAPITAL OF SOUTHEAST ASIA

During the 1970s and early 1980s, under a controversial iron-fisted democracy, Singapore's economy expanded at an annual rate of nearly 9 percent. Booming manufacturing and service sectors have helped Singapore's nearly 3 million people to gain an average income of $15,000, close to the level of western Europe's wealthiest nations. And Singapore has developed new lines of business that assure its growth in the 1990s; it has emerged as the financial and technological hub of southeast Asia.

EQUITIES IN SINGAPORE

Equities trade on the Stock Exchange of Singapore (SES). Through 1993, the Straits Times Industrial Index was up 59 percent. Investors may have based their decision on the favorable economic outlook expected by supranational lending agencies, such as The Asian Development Bank (ADB), which sees continued high growth and low inflation for Singapore throughout 1995. The Singapore government is assisting the trend to higher prices; it wants its citizens to invest. The government ran a month-long advertising campaign in 1993 to explain to Singaporeans how to buy stocks and announced new rules that make it easier for them to do so. The government, for example, doubled the amount of Social Security funds that individuals can earmark for local stocks.

One reason for the promotional effort stems from government plans to privatize large state-controlled businesses. The government wants to ensure the same success for upcoming privatizations as it had with **Singapore Telecommunications Pte.**, which is the sole provider of local and international telecommunications and postal services for the island nation. Though priced at 50 times earnings (versus an overall P/E ratio of 22 for the SES), the multi-billion-dollar offering was 3.5 times oversubscribed, thanks to foreign institutional investors—testament to the bullish future they see for Singapore.

CURRENCY OUTLOOK

Investing in stocks with Singapore dollars has been an added plus. From 1987 to 1994, the Singapore dollar rose on average 2 to 5 percent a year compared with the U.S. dollar, adding that much to an international investor's gains. This trend should continue in 1995.

SOUTH AFRICA

Buy

INVESTMENT FACTORS

	1993	1994E
Real Economic Growth:	1.0%	2.5%
Inflation:	9.0%	9.5%
Current Account (% of GDP):	0.5%	0.0%

Politics: In April 1994, for the first time, every adult South African was able to vote in a national election. A peaceful move to majority rule will encourage investor confidence and boost infrastructure projects that drive growth. Caution: Violence at any time could postpone economic gains.

STOCK MARKET OUTLOOK

Though events following the election carry a near-term risk to investors, this market has good long-term prospects. The country is rich with gold and other natural resources that have been increasing in price. Indeed, the Johannesburg Gold Stock Index was up 171 percent in 1993, from depressed levels, while its Industrials Index was up 28 percent. More important is that institutional investors in the United States and other countries, who are diversifying abroad and who have been barred from owning South African equities, are expected to give a strong underpinning to the market, given the smooth transfer of political power.

STOCKS TO CONSIDER

The American Depositary Receipts (ADRs) of eighteen South African stocks, mostly gold-mining companies, are traded on NASDAQ. Here are five to consider buying:

- **Anglo American Corp.** (NASDAQ: ANGLY) Some consider this well-known giant industrial concern to have such diverse holdings that it is practically a substitute for a South African country fund. The firm has committed $1.7 billion to six major new ventures in South Africa and abroad.
- **Barlow Rand** (OTC: BRRAY) South Africa's largest indus-

trial group in terms of sales and assets controls major subsidiaries in packaging, textiles, food, and pharmaceuticals, as
well as mining.

- **De Beers Consolidated** (NASDAQ: DBRSY) De Beers markets 80 percent of the world's rough-cut diamonds, which are
showing some price improvement. This is perhaps the world's
most familiar mining and gold stock. With high cash generation
and a strong balance sheet, these shares should grow significantly.
- **Gencor Industries** (NASDAQ: GCOR) South Africa's second-largest mining concern plans to "unbundle" subsidiaries
that are valued at a discount to asset value by giving shareholders in the parent company shares in the companies that
are spun off. The value of the parts should sum up to more
than the whole.
- **South African Breweries** (OTC: SABLY) Considered a
blue-chip conglomerate, it operates hotels, wineries, and furniture and department stores. It also sells 98 percent of the beer
in South Africa.

CLOSED-END FUNDS

Looking for a South Africa country fund? You won't have long to
wait—three or four are on the way. They're likely to be very popular, but *do not pay a premium for them*. Because several are in the off-
ing, none is likely to sustain a premium price for long. Check the
Wall Street Journal or ask your broker to make sure that you do not
pay above the Net Asset Value for such closed-end shares.

OVERVIEW

Not too long ago, investing in South Africa was an emotionally
charged issue, but now even "socially responsible" funds can profit

there in clear conscience. What's more, there is a good chance that South Africa will turn out to be one of the top-performing emerging markets in years to come. In September 1993, the United States and the United Nations began lifting financial and economic sanctions against South Africa, and global portfolio managers regained interest in buying equities there because the prospects for economic growth are excellent. While U.S. institutional investors are faced with the largely unquantifiable risk of how smooth the country's transition to a multiracial democracy will be, they now have a political green light to invest, and they want to focus some cash there. That is good news for individual investors who want to buy South African stocks, since U.S. pension funds are starting from scratch.

How much might the institutions buy? For comparison, consider the total value of stocks that U.S. investors have purchased in Australia, a country with comparable resources and a similarly sized market to South Africa. It is estimated that U.S. investors own nearly $4 billion of Australia's equities. To reach that level in South Africa, institutional investors will have to be consistent buyers of South African equities for years to come. One problem for pension funds, though: It could take most of 1995 to overturn all the legislation in 166 state, county, and city jurisdictions across the country that blocks them from owning South African stocks and bonds. No such rules restrict individuals, who can invest ahead of the herd.

Changing Political Climate Boosts Stocks

South African equities trade on the 107-year-old Johannesburg Stock Exchange, where the lifting of sanctions had a positive effect on prices. With U.S. institutional investors cautiously entering the market, South Africa's stock market was worth nearly $200 billion, just behind Switzerland's. In fact, South Africa is the largest "emerging" market besides Hong Kong ($231 billion).

Well Endowed with Natural Resources

An upswing in the world economy will fuel demand for South Africa's abundance of mineral resources, which include:

- 25 percent of the world's diamonds
- 44 percent of the world's gold reserves
- 69 percent of the world's platinum group metals

CURRENCY OUTLOOK

South Africa has two currencies, the commercial rand, used by its citizens, and the financial rand, which foreigners use to buy stocks and bonds at a discount. Typically, the financial rand is cheaper than the commercial rand is. Investors are allowed to convert dividends and interest back into dollars at the higher commercial rand rate. In 1993, that turned South Africa's 13 percent bond interest into a 16 percent yield for foreign investors. This "bonus" is an incentive for foreigners to hold South African investments during turbulent times and most likely will not be available when the political situation calms down, months or years from now. Naturally when foreign investors liquidate a stock or bond holding, their rands get converted back to dollars through the financial rand; otherwise, foreign investors could simply buy the cheaper currency and sell the more expensive one (via a simultaneous investment purchase and sale) for a riskless profit. While the financial rand's discount to the commercial rand fluctuates daily—in 1986 it was as low as 50 percent—with foreign investment on its way in, the financial rand's discount, if anything, should narrow compared with the commercial rand and thus add to your profits if you buy your investments there with financial rand.

SOUTH AFRICA'S LONG-TERM CHALLENGE

With per capita income at $2,500 a year, the World Bank considers South Africa to be in the upper-middle-income bracket of developing countries, but disparities inside the nation are enormous. White incomes are estimated, for example, to be ten times those of blacks. In addition, private South African capital has been fleeing the country at a rate of $1 billion to $2 billion a year. South Africa must reactivate the private sector, increase employment, and narrow the difference in incomes between blacks and whites. To do that and achieve sustainable economic growth, South Africa needs to attract substantial investment from outside the country.

INVESTMENT RISKS

Even with the smoothest transfer of political power that followed the national election on April 27, 1994, many large international investors are still hesitating to make investments in South Africa. The transition to a multiracial democracy will not fully take hold for years, yet investment results in the interim will depend on political and social developments that could prove tumultuous.

- Civil Disturbance. The ongoing risks of social disruption in South Africa will keep some investors from making investments there. Prior to the national elections, the Zulu-based Inkatha Freedom Party as well as the Afrikaner Volksfront (a group of conservative white political parties) showed their disapproval of constitutional changes through acts of violence. They may not quietly disappear from the horizon.
- Currency Risk. It is anticipated that the new government will come under strong pressure to relax monetary and fiscal policy in order to stimulate the economy. If this is mismanaged, the financial (and commercial) rand could decline in value against the dollar, thus reducing returns or even causing a loss for foreign investors.

AN IRONY OF SANCTIONS: SOUTH AFRICA IS COMPARATIVELY DEBT FREE

As a consequence of economic sanctions, many international banks were barred from lending money to South Africa, leaving the country to make ends meet for itself. Thus South Africa has relatively little foreign debt—15 percent of GDP compared with an average of over 100 percent of GDP for sub-Saharan African countries. This will make it easier for the country to obtain needed financing, and several supranational lending agencies, such as the International Monetary Authority (IMF) and the International Bank for Reconstruction and Development (IBRD), intend on making financing available. The IBRD loans are slated for infrastructure development—health, education, housing, and transportation—which, along with improving lives, will improve South African labor productivity. Not all multinational firms will come back, but some will, providing jobs and investment. And many governments have pledged financial and technical assistance to aid the country's political transition.

SPAIN

Hold

INVESTMENT FACTORS

	1993	*1994*E
Real Economic Growth:	-1.1%	1.5%
Inflation:	4.5%	4.0%
Current Account (% of GDP):	-2.5%	-1.0%
3-month Peseta deposits:	11.5%	8.0%
10-year bond yields:	10.5%	10.00%

Political: Felipe Gonzalez, the prime minister since 1982, barely won the 1993 election. The main issues were Spain's 22 percent unemployment rate—Western Europe's highest—and a growing budget deficit muddied by corruption scandals.

STOCK MARKET OUTLOOK

Spanish stocks are likely to be good investments for those with a three- to five-year perspective. Lower Spanish interest rates will help the market move higher in 1995, and then there may be a pause, unless economic growth takes place within three to six months.

STOCKS TO CONSIDER

- **Empresa Nacional de Electricidad** (NYSE: ELE) Spain's largest producer of electricity will benefit from falling interest rates. It has good cash flow and a strong balance sheet that should allow it to perform above average when the economy turns around. As of December 1993, the dividend yield was 2.4 percent.
- **Repsol, S.A.** (NYSE: REP) Spain's petrochemical company has been aggressive in its exploration for and production of oil and gas in Spain and in Africa and Indonesia. Earnings have been more stable than at most U.S. companies. Repsol purchased a 45 percent interest in a gas supply company and now supplies 90 percent of Spain's gas customers.
- **Telefonica de Espana** (NYSE: TEF) Controls all domestic

and international phone service in Spain. As of late 1994, its dividend yielded about 3.3 percent. TEF is expanding into Europe. Earnings have been erratic but should improve when Spain's economy does. A long-term hold.

CLOSED-END SPANISH FUNDS

- **First Iberian Fund** (NYSE: IBF) Invests in securities in Spain and Portugal, with about 80 percent of its assets in Spain. Solid growth in recent years.
- **Spain Fund** (NYSE: SNF) Invests at least 65 percent of its assets in Spanish equities, with the balance in peseta-denominated fixed-income securities. Expected to post good returns.

OVERVIEW

After joining the European Community (EC) in 1986, Spain lowered trade barriers and liberalized its capital markets. Foreign and domestic investment spurred average growth to 4 percent, and until 1991, Spain had Europe's most dynamic economy. Then came the recession that affected all of Europe, and one out of five Spaniards was out of work. Despite this, of all the "new" entrants to the EC, Spain offers international investors the best long-term prospects of dramatically raising its economic performance toward the level of such EC members as France and the U.K. Spanish equities trade on the Madrid Stock Exchange, and the stock market rose 51 percent through 1993, despite the economy's shrinking by 1 percent; 1994 results were slightly less impressive. The stock market performance spurred several Spanish companies to list American Depository Receipts (ADRs) on the New York Stock Exchange.

The challenge facing Spain is to successfully adjust its economy to the competitive single European market. This will take time, but bet on Spain to pull it off. Consider how this economy has progressed through a century of change:

- 1950: Agriculture-based Economy
Until the 1950s, Spain's economy was predominantly agricultural.

- 1960s and 1970s: Industrial Isolation
During the 1960s and 70s, Francisco Franco, Spain's dictator, attempted to build a completely independent economy by cutting imports and rapidly expanding industries from petroleum and steel to automobiles and chemicals.

- 1986: Global Competition
EC membership gave Spain access to world markets.

A KING, A SOCIALIST, AND THE CORTES

General Franco was a royalist, but it was not until after his death in 1975 that a new reign began. Then, after nearly a half century without a king, Carlos I became Spain's hereditary chief executive. Political power, however, rests with the Cortes (the national assembly), which consists of an appointed Senate and a freely elected lower house, the congress of Deputies, most of whose members are from Spain's socialist party.

SUCCESSFUL PRIVATIZATIONS WITH MORE COMING

Though philosophically against extensive privatizations, Spain's socialist government has begun to sell state assets in order to reduce the country's large budget deficit and to increase industrial productivity. In 1993, Madrid raised more than $1 billion by selling off a 25 percent stake in Argentaria, the state-controlled banking conglomerate, while retaining a 75 percent interest. International investors oversubscribed the offer, and by August the shares had soared 60 percent above the initial offering price. Upcoming privatizations include top-rated utilities, a giant shipping concern, and Tabacalera, the state tobacco monopoly.

GOVERNMENT INITIATIVES WILL HELP CERTAIN INDUSTRIES

To reactivate the economy, the government increased spending on major infrastructure projects; public works contracts increased 80 percent in 1993 over the year previous. The stocks of companies in the building and materials industries will benefit.

Spanish interest rates reached record levels of around 12 percent in 1993. Analysts expect these rates to fall to 8 percent through 1995, boosting the prospects of banks' stocks as well as the chances of a general economic recovery.

The government allowed its currency, the peseta, to depreciate by 27 percent against the German D-mark and 25 percent against the U.S. dollar, boosting its exports and attracting tourists. *Note:* Tourism is the single most important international sector for Spain. Tourism revenues hover around 2.1 trillion pesetas versus 6.1 trillion for all merchandise exports combined.

BOND AND CURRENCY OUTLOOK

Spanish bonds will likely rise in price as the economy continues in recession, but the peseta remains vulnerable; expect it to decline 10 percent to 15 percent in 1994-1995. Consider an international bond fund with Spanish holdings that hedges substantially all its currency risk. Three such mutual funds are listed below.

	RETURNS AS OF 8/30/93				% of Peseta Risk Hedged
	1-Year	3-Year	5-Year	% in Spain	
• Global Government Plus	14.64%	12.68%	11.61%	15%	100%
• Global Income Plus	9.51%	10.47%	N/A	12%	100%
• Global Yield	11.57%	8.55%	9.45%	10%	100%

SWITZERLAND

Buy

INVESTMENT FACTORS

	1993	*1994*E
Real Economic Growth:	-0.5%	2.0%
Inflation:	3.0%	2.0%
Current Account (% of GDP):	7.5%	6.5%
3-month Swiss franc deposits:	5.0%	4.0%
10-year bond yields:	4.5%	5.0%

Economic: Switzerland came out of recession a bit ahead of its European neighbors, but expect the Swiss recovery to continue at a gradual pace because of weak European demand for its exports. Inflation will likely continue downward as unemployment reaches a very un-Swiss 5 percent.

STOCK MARKET OUTLOOK

The Swiss Price Index was up 40 percent in 1993, in line with the other large market gains throughout Europe. The Swiss stock market should perform relatively well, compared with Germany and France, in 1995. First, Switzerland does not have the unsustainable high costs that German manufacturers have, and Switzerland does not have to restructure state-owned companies the way France does. Also, the Swiss are running a historically high current account, which means that increased profits are being generated by Swiss companies abroad. That favors its currency and stock market.

STOCKS TO CONSIDER

The drawbacks to investing directly in Swiss shares make the foreign investor better off sticking with a mutual fund when investing there. Stock commissions are high for individual investors in Switzerland, and Swiss stock selection is complicated by the fact that there are classes of stocks (such as bearer certificates), which are not found on U.S. exchanges. In addition, Switzerland does not have a version of the U.S. Securities and Exchange Commission to oversee its markets.

A Closed-end Fund That Invests in Switzerland

	12/31/93 Price	Premium	Annual Returns 3-year	Annual Returns 1-year	% of Assets in Switzerland
Europe Fund (EF)	$13	2.0%	11.5%	41.9%	20

Open-end Funds with Investments in Switzerland

Fidelity Europe (nl)			6.7%	27.16%	9
Vanguard Int'l Equity Index-Europe (1% load)			9.8%	29.13%	11

Data from Morningstar.

Overview

Nestled in the heart of Europe, surrounded by the Alps, Switzerland is an economic Shangri-la where the standard of living, per capita output, education, science, and health care are unsurpassed. Switzerland has prospered amidst the rapidly changing political and economic situation in eastern Europe, as well as the ongoing integration of western Europe; but not because the Swiss have hidden behind their mountains. Swiss multinational corporations are among the world's largest pharmaceutical, insurance, construction, and, of course, banking companies in the world. It is the international earnings which those companies bring home that support Europe's highest living standards. How green is the grass over there? Well, economic growth typically runs between 1 and 3 percent annually (as in the United States), but that's where the similarity ends.

- The federal budget is, on average, in balance.
- There is relatively little unemployment, less than 2.0 percent.
- Inflation is low.
- The country runs a current account surplus, meaning that the Swiss sell more goods and services abroad than they import. In fact, as a percent of their economic output, the Swiss have twice as high a surplus as the Japanese. (And none of Switzerland's trading partners mind!)

THE ZURICH STOCK MARKET

There are regional exchanges in Basle and Geneva, but most Swiss equities are listed on the Zurich Stock Exchange. Although Switzerland is only one-thirteenth the size of France, its stock market is the fourth largest in Europe, following those of London, Frankfurt and Paris. The Swiss Price Index (SPI) monitors the performance of the overall stock market and was up 40 percent for 1993. This trend is expected to moderate somewhat in 1994-95.

4

SWISS CORPORATIONS COMPETE GLOBALLY

Many Swiss corporations are top global competitors in their fields. Diversified across a broad number of geographic markets and producing numerous products, these companies are less vulnerable than most to economic downturns.

Construction:	**BBC Brown Boveri**
Finance/Banking:	**Credit Suisse Holding**
	Swiss Bank Corporation
	Union Bank of Switzerland
Insurance:	**Swiss Reinsurance**
	Winterthur Insurance
Packaged Food/	
Consumer Goods:	**Nestle**
Pharmaceuticals:	**Ciba Geigy**
	Sandoz

SWISS MULTINATIONAL CORPORATIONS: A GLOBAL PLAY

How can you accrue part of the profits the Swiss make? One way is to own shares in their large multinational corporations. Though the domestic Swiss economy is growing, it is of secondary importance to the performance of these Swiss giants, many of which record total annual sales in excess of Switzerland's entire GDP. Consider just how global they are:

- The ten largest Swiss industrial companies obtain less than 10 percent of their total sales within Switzerland.
- Swiss insurance companies receive 65 percent of their premium income from outside the country.
- More than half of Swiss banking revenues come from overseas.

CURRENCY OUTLOOK

The Swiss franc is likely to weaken 5 to 8 percent against the U.S. dollar in 1995, which means that the franc will actually strengthen against the currencies of Europe. The D-mark, for instance, is expected to fall 10 to 15 percent against the U.S. dollar in 1995. One reason: The Swiss National Bank is not expected to lower interest rates as much as the Bundesbank.

SWISS CORPORATE EARNINGS ARE INSULATED FROM CURRENCY RISK

If, from one year to the next, the dollar trades 10 percent higher against the Swiss franc, then the dollar profits of a Swiss company will translate into 10 percent more Swiss francs back in Switzerland. Because more than half of the total profits of Swiss multinational corporations are typically earned overseas, a weaker Swiss franc actually increases the profits of Swiss companies.

TAIWAN

Buy

INVESTMENT FACTORS

	1993	1994E
Real Economic Growth:	6.0%	6.5%
Inflation:	3.5%	4.0%
Current Account (% of GDP):	3.0%	2.0%

Politics: The growing importance of mainland China's economy is causing Taiwan to rethink its restrictions on foreign investors. In 1994 Taiwan increased the amount of foreign money allowed into the country's stock market. That should lead to an increase in share prices on the Taiwan Stock Exchange.

STOCK MARKET OUTLOOK

Given that Taiwan's market leapt ahead 80 percent in 1993, one might have expected a pullback in 1994. And indeed that's what happened. This has created buying opportunities for the long-term. Thanks to continued export growth to China, Taiwan's economy should maintain a 6 percent growth rate through 1995.

CLOSED-END FUNDS THAT INVEST IN TAIWAN

	12/31/93 Price	Premium	Annual Returns 3-year	Annual Returns 1-year
R.O.C. Taiwan (NYSE: ROC)	$13-3/4	29.5%	20%	59%
Taiwan Fund (NYSE: TWN)	37-7/8	46.4%	39%	99%

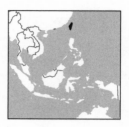

OVERVIEW

Taiwan is an island located 115 miles off the southeast coast of China. In 1949, when the communists took over mainland China, Taiwan became the last refuge of the Chinese Nationalist Party (the Kuomintang). Since then the Nationalists have officially sought "recovery of the mainland," though they have become less vocal as mainland China becomes more prosperous and powerful. With 21 million people, Taiwan has less than 2 percent of China's population and does not want to provoke Beijing, which claims Taiwan as one of its provinces.

Taiwan is diplomatically isolated; few countries recognize it as a separate country, including the United States, which since 1978 has had a one-China policy that recognizes Beijing. Still, Taiwan out-muscles the mainland in per capita economic output. The average Taiwanese produces $10,600 worth of goods and services each year, as compared with China's average output per person of $400.

A DYNAMIC CAPITALIST ECONOMY

- Real economic growth in Taiwan averaged almost 9 percent a year from 1960 through 1990. Despite all the political rhetoric, Taiwan's swift economic growth has been aided by a dramatic expansion of its trade with and investment in China.
- Taiwan shipped $200 million worth of goods to China in 1982, $800 million worth in 1986, and $4.6 billion worth in 1991—and the trend continues.
- Taiwan businesses have shifted labor-intensive industries to the mainland, where wages are one-sixth the level in Taiwan. That has made Taiwan a major investor in China.

AN INVESTMENT STRATEGY FOR TAIWAN

Given the current regulatory environment in Taiwan, the closed-end Taiwan funds are the best way to play this market. Just watch their premium-to-portfolio value. Buy when the premium goes down to 10 percent or 20 percent; usually the price is down at this time also.

FOREIGN INVESTORS WILL BE MORE WELCOME

Equities trade on the Taiwan Stock Exchange in Taipei. Two closed-end Taiwan funds trade on the New York Stock Exchange; **R.O.C. Taiwan** (ROC), and the **Taiwan Fund** (TWN). Taiwan tightly restricts the amount of foreign investments—foreigners can own no more than $5 billion worth of Taiwan shares, or just 4 percent of the market's $120 billion value. Hopes for a further liberalization of foreign investment rules will help the market though such hopes have been dashed before. This time supporters of such measures include the government, which craves global recognition as a tactic to ensure its main objective: Taiwan's independence from China. Taiwan badly wants to become a member of GATT, the group of nations that sets rules on global trade and tariffs, and GATT favors a lifting of restrictions on Taiwan's international capital flows. Also, Taiwan's government wants Taipei to become a regional financial center, but Taipei cannot become "the next Hong Kong" until it reduces or abolishes foreign investment restrictions.

THAILAND

Buy

INVESTMENT FACTORS

	1993	1994E
Real Economic Growth:	7.0%	8.0%
Inflation:	3.5%	4.5%
Current Account (% of GDP):	-6.5%	-5.0%

Economic: Thailand's economic growth is expected to remain strong in 1995. Lower interest rates, along with inflows of foreign capital and spending on infrastructure, will support the economy. Indeed, if anything can slow this new Asian tiger it is that solutions to infrastructure problems, such as water shortages and insufficient mass transit, will not keep pace with growth.

STOCK MARKET OUTLOOK

Although stock prices on the Securities Exchange of Thailand shot up 88 percent in 1993, do not expect this market to proceed in a straight line up—10 percent and 20 percent corrections will be the norm—but the three- to five-year prognosis is for continued strong performance.

CLOSED-END FUNDS THAT INVEST IN THAILAND

12/31/93	Price	Premium	Annual Returns 3-year	1-year	% of Assets in Thailand
Asia Pacific (NYSE: APB)	$25-1/2	19.5%	53%	123%	15
Scudder New Asia (NYSE: SAF)	$27-3/8	N/A	36%	95%	12

OPEN-END FUNDS WITH INVESTMENTS IN THAILAND

GAM Pacific Basin (5% load)			22.38%	63.91%	10
Merrill Lynch Dragon (4% load)			28.16%	68.96%	11

Scudder Pacific   33.37%   60.08%   7
Opportunities (nl)

   Data from Morningstar.

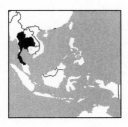

OVERVIEW

Bangkok is a nineteen-hour flight from New York. If you make the trip, expect to land in a tropical boom town. Between 1986 and 1993, Thailand's economy grew almost 8.5 percent a year, and the country's infrastructure has not kept pace. That is why the government is laying telecommunications lines and building roads and port facilities, all of which are adding to Thailand's prospects for continued strong growth in 1995–96.

THE THAI STOCK MARKET HAS GROWN DRAMATICALLY

In 1980, Thailand's stock market, The Securities Exchange of Thailand (SET), was worth less than $1 billion. The total value of stocks now listed on SET is more than $60 billion. Consider what has been fueling this growth and you can see why Thailand's general economic outlook is excellent.

- Thailand has an increasingly sophisticated export-oriented manufacturing sector, supported by high levels of foreign business investment, particularly from Japan.
- It is a food exporter to the world's most populous region.
- Extensive natural gas and petroleum deposits are being developed and will reduce oil imports.
- Inflation is running less than 3.5 percent.
- Thailand's currency, the baht, has been stable; since 1987, it has ranged in value between 25 and 26 bahts per U.S. dollar.

- Increased tax receipts from the fast-moving economy helped Bangkok record its sixth consecutive budget surplus.

CURRENCY OUTLOOK

In the world of currency trading, Thailand's currency, the baht, has remained remarkably stable against the U.S. dollar, averaging close to 4 cents each year since the mid-1980s. Steady as she goes in 1995.

POLITICAL CHAOS APPEARS TO BE AT AN END

Thailand's economy has grown rapidly despite a succession of recent governments and upheavals such as the military's shooting of anti-government demonstrators in May 1992. However, after five governments in three years, a stable civilian-led administration took office in 1992. This has encouraged confidence in the Thai equity market, which has trended upwards.

AN INVESTMENT STRATEGY FOR THAILAND

Until the late 1980s, Thailand was unknown to international investors. Partly because of that, there are few easy routes for foreign individuals to purchase Thai stock directly. The best bet is to invest a closed-end fund or a mutual fund with investments in Thailand. This provides diversification among many issues, which spreads the investment risk and provides for stock selection by professionals who focus on Thailand and the region.

UNITED KINGDOM
Buy

INVESTMENT FACTORS

	1993	1994E
Real Economic Growth:	1.8%	3.5%
Inflation:	2.0%	2.5%
Current Account (% of GDP):	-2.0%	-2.0%
3-month Sterling deposits:	6.0%	5.5%
10-year bond yields:	7.5%	8.0%

Economics: The U.K. broke ranks with Europe's high-interest-rate policy in late 1992 and has been reaping the benefits ever since. While the continent is just climbing out of recession, the U.K. has been growing for over a year. Growth will remain stable in 1995 and possibly pick up a bit in the second half of the year.

STOCK MARKET OUTLOOK

London's stock market should be an above-average performer in the next three to five years. The FTSE (Financial Times Stock Exchange) 100-share index ended 1993 at 3,418, just short of the record high set the day before and well ahead of the world's two other most liquid markets (the U.S. S&P 500 index rose 7.1%, and Tokyo's Nikkei rose 3%). In addition to a growing economy supporting stronger stock prices, the sheer size of London's market and the international stocks there will likely make this market attractive to American institutions looking to diversify their holdings abroad.

STOCKS TO CONSIDER
- **Glaxo Holdings** (NYSE: GLX) Britain's largest drug company and the second largest in the world. It is the producer of Zantac, the blockbuster anti-ulcer drug. New products are continually coming on line and should keep Glaxo a strong competitor.
- **Reuters** (OTC: RTRSY) The world's largest electronic publisher provides business news and market prices on securities and currencies around the world. Has a very strong cash flow,

which allows it to expand easily. The company will boost earnings about 20 percent in 1994. Will be right on the scene as the European economies recover.

A Closed-end U.K. Fund

- **United Kingdom Fund** (NYSE: UKM) Invests at least 65 percent of its assets in U.K. stocks, particularly smaller company stocks. A small cap bull market is expected as the U.K. recovers.

Overview

Between the Tower of London and St. Paul's Cathedral is one square mile that once contained the medieval city of London. That area is still known as "the City" and now holds the U.K.'s version of Wall Street. Britain is the largest foreign owner of U.S. stocks, bonds, and real estate. The reverse is also true—American corporations and individuals are the largest foreign owners of British financial assets. More American bankers and brokers work in London than anywhere else outside the United States, which is one reason why buying U.K. stock or bonds is almost as easy as investing at home in the United States.

The International Stock Exchange

London has Europe's most vibrant financial center, and the global portion of its business is growing. Of the 3,000-plus companies listed on its exchange, more than 500 are headquartered outside the U.K. It was with good reason that the London Stock Exchange changed its name to the International Stock Exchange (ISE).

- The U.K. equities market is the third largest in the world, after the United States and Japan.

- And though the U.K. economy ranks as the fourth largest in Europe, its stock market is larger than the Frankfurt, Paris, and Milan markets combined.

The "Footsie 100"

The most commonly quoted measure of London's equities is the FTSE 100 index, commonly known as the "Footsie 100." Designed by the *Financial Times* (FT) and the Stock Exchange (SE), it comprises the top 100 U.K. companies, which account for approximately 70 percent of the market.

One of the World's Great Trading Nations

As a major trading nation, the U.K. has an economy that is sensitive to patterns of growth or recession worldwide. However, the U.K. is remarkably self-sufficient compared with Japan or Germany. It produces 60 percent of its own food needs and is an energy-rich nation with large coal, natural gas, and oil reserves. *The U.K. is an oil exporter*, which means that if oil prices climb, its economy will be insulated and may even prosper, while other industrialized countries will be relatively worse off.

Bond Market Outlook

Although the big gains in the U.K.'s bond market are over, one positive for bonds is that economic growth is slow at 2 percent, allowing interest rates to remain low, but inflation may inch up in 1995–96. This is a negative for bond prices.

Currency Outlook

The British pound will probably suffer less than its European counterparts in 1995 declining by 6 to 12 percent. In fact, the pound, which took so much abuse in late 1992, has actually been strengthening against other European currencies.

In September 1992, Britain pulled out of Europe's Exchange Rate Mechanism, which allowed its currency, the Pound Sterling, to fall against other European currencies. At the core of this decision was Britain's resolve to set its own interest rates according to British needs and not according to the monetary policies of its European trading partners. In hindsight, it was an astute decision that allowed the U.K. to immediately lower interest rates and stimulate economic activity. At the time, the pound fell precipitously (that was when George Soros made headlines by reportedly making over one billion dollars selling the pound). However, in 1993, while other European countries remained mired in recession—forced to maintain high interest rates to keep their currencies from falling against the German D-mark—Britain's economy was already growing. With these improving economic fundamentals, the pound is expected to remain stable or to increase in value against the currencies of its trading partners during 1995–96.

VENEZUELA

Stay Away

INVESTMENT FACTORS

	1993	*1994*E
Real Economic Growth:	-2.0%	-0.5%
Inflation:	45.0%	70.0%
Current Account (% of GDP):	-2.0%	-4.0%

Political: Rumors of coup attempts by Venezuela's military marred an otherwise smooth December 1993 election of President Rafael Caldera, one of the candidates the military did not support.

STOCK MARKET OUTLOOK

Venezuela's new president, Rafael Caldera, has pledged fiscal austerity but is reluctant to raise taxes. With oil prices extremely volatile, Venezuela's oil revenues are likely to decline. Expect a worsening federal deficit, which will hold back economic growth. Net result for equities will be sideways to lower.

LATIN AMERICAN OPEN-END MUTUAL FUNDS

If Venezuela turns around, or if a profitable investment opportunity arises there, the chances are the investment professionals specializing in the region will spot it first. Here are three open-end mutual funds to consider that invest in the region.

TOTAL RETURNS THROUGH 12/31/93
- G.T. Latin America Growth   52.94%
- Merrill Lynch Latin America   63.05%
- Scudder Latin America   74.32%

OVERVIEW

Venezuela's politics have been in turmoil. In February and November 1992, two unsuccessful military coups rocked the nation and the confidence of international investors. Then in May 1993, President Carlos Perez was impeached for alleged embezzlement of public funds. Next, a former president, Jaime Lusinchi (1984–89), was indicted for the same crime. Some relief came on December 5, 1993, when Venezuelans peacefully elected populist candidate Rafael Caldera, seventy-seven years old, as president. He had previously been president, from 1969 to 1974.

ECONOMIC DIFFICULTIES

Venezuela's economy took a tumble in 1993, partly because of the country's political turmoil. After growing 10 percent in 1991 and 7 percent in 1992, the economy fell 2 percent in 1993; 1994 was not much better. Venezuela has not taken economic reforms as far as Argentina and Chile. For instance, inflation was over 40 percent in 1993, and the government's fiscal deficit increased from an average 3 percent of Gross Domestic Product (GDP) between 1986 and 1991, to 5 percent of GDP in 1993.

VENEZUELAN STOCKS

Equities trade on the Caracas Stock Exchange. From 1989 through 1991, the exchange grew explosively from a total value of $1.5 billion to $13 billion, but with the onset of weaker economic results and political unrest, the market dropped back down to a value of approximately $8 billion in 1992. For 1993, the Caracas market was down 20 percent in U.S. dollar terms.

TOO DEPENDENT ON OIL EXPORTS

Venezuela is South America's biggest oil exporter, but in an era of fluctating oil prices that can be a problem because oil still represents 80 percent of the country's export revenues. A lower price for oil substantially reduces government revenues, and consequently increases its fiscal deficit increased. By contrast, Mexico, which used to be overly dependent on oil fifteen to twenty years ago, has successfully diversified its economy since—oil is down to 30 percent of total output in Mexico—and so it is not as vulnerable as Venezuela to a lower price of oil.

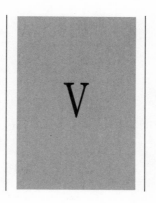

OTHER GLOBAL OPPORTUNITIES

CHAPTER TWELVE

MAKING MONEY IN FOREIGN CURRENCIES

The price of one currency in terms of another is its "Foreign Exchange Rate." The term "Exchange" relates to the physical delivery of one currency against payment in another. In this chapter we show how you can profit from switching some of your savings into a foreign currency Certificate of Deposit (CD) or a Foreign Money Market Fund. While the news media have reported on the mega-profits of such foreign currency speculators as George Soros, who in 1992 reportedly made $1.5 billion selling the British pound, we want to say right now that their methods are *not* covered in this chapter. Investing in currencies differs from fast-paced professional currency trading in the way driving a station wagon differs from pressing the pedal to the metal of an Indy 500 race car. The holding period for our currency investments ranges from two months to two years, but to a speculator, two weeks can seem forever.

WHY BUY A FOREIGN CURRENCY

- *Higher Rates of Return.* The interest paid on a number of foreign currency deposits and money market funds is more than twice what you can earn on U.S. dollars. If a foreign currency remains stable compared to the dollar (see below), you can capture this higher return.

- *Safety.* If the dollar threatens to collapse, it will be important to know how to get some of your savings into another currency. An unlikely event? Yes, but history is full of examples of currencies that have devalued dramatically, leaving savers "financially landlocked." For example, in 1982, the U.S. dollar-Mexican peso exchange rate broke free of its fixed rate of U.S. $1.00 = M.P. 25.00 and fell to U.S. $1.00 = M.P. 500, which left Mexicans essentially unable to move their money into another currency. First, the post-devaluation exchange rate made it too expensive ($100,000 worth of pesos was now worth only $5,000), then in order to prevent a further collapse of their currency, the Mexican government imposed "exchange control" regulations that prohibited such transactions, making it a crime for investors to sell pesos to buy dollars.

- *Opportunity.* Currencies often move in steady long-term trends, which allows investors plenty of time to buy into and sell out positions for a profit. The Japanese yen rose 17% during the first half of 1993. The dollar soared in the early Reagan years, gaining 46% against the German mark from November 1980 to February 1985.

- *Low Volatility.* Even in 1992, prices of the major currencies fluctuated far less than those of stocks and bonds. The investments we will recommend are less risky than owning U.S. stocks or bonds.

1

UP AND DOWN THE DOLLAR

Think of an exchange rate as a ratio of two currencies. Around the world, the dollar moves up or down in value as *compared to* another currency, and the following relationships occur.

If the U.S. dollar goes up, the value of a foreign currency goes down, and:

- Foreign goods become cheaper.
- U.S. imports increase.

If the U.S. dollar goes down, the value of a foreign currency goes up, and:

- U.S. goods become cheaper.
- U.S. exports increase.

CURRENCIES FOR INVESTMENT

The following currencies account for more than 75% of all the trading volume in currencies. Several major currencies are not on the list, most notably the French franc; over the last decade the French government has established or threatened to create restrictions and tariffs on foreigners investing in their currency.

Note: If family connections, work, or travel gives you access to an additional currency that is not on our list but that fits our criteria, you can add it to the list. The analysis that follows will still apply.

2

CURRENCY	ALIAS	TRADING RANGES	
		1993	1990-93
British Pound	Sterling	$1.4008–1.5904	$1.4008–1.9920
Canadian Dollar	Canada,		
	Spot Funds	.7401–.8017	.7401–.8906
German Mark	deutschemark,		
	D-Mark	.5702–.6351	.5401–.7145
Japanese Yen	Yen	.7915–.9959	.6254–.9959
Swiss Franc	Swissy	.6405–.7212	.6254–.8209

Source: IMM, through 12/31/93. Quoted in U.S. dollars per foreign currency, except for the yen, which is per 100 yen.

3
MEXICAN PESO: AN EXCEPTION TO THE RULE

Although the Mexican peso is not a major currency, it is worth considering now for investment. Here's why: Mexican inflation has been falling, its currency has been relatively stable, and Mexican three-month Treasury bills (CETES) pay high interest. The goal is to earn substantially more peso interest than you lose on the exchange rate. In mid-1993, Mexican inflation was below 10 percent, three-month CETES paid 16 percent, and the peso was declining at a 7 percent annual rate. To figure your total yield in dollars, subtract the 7 percent loss on the peso-dollar exchange rate from the 16 percent peso interest. You still pick up 9%. This abnormally high return should continue through 1994, due in part to increased U.S. corporate investment in Mexico, which will help bolster the peso. Mexico has been on its best financial behavior to encourage this trend. A reversal on the inflation front would be a signal to get out.

Mexican Brokers to contact for more information on buying Mexican Treasury bills:

> Inverlat International (212) 804-4100
>
> InverMexico U.S.A. (212) 683-7575
>
> Probursa International (212) 949-8855
>
> Serfin Securities Inc. (212) 750-4200

A MUTUAL FUND THAT BUYS MEXICAN TREASURY BILLS

Dean Witter markets a mutual fund, the *North American Government Income Fund* run by Trust Company of the West (TC West), which invests up to 25 percent of the fund's assets in Mexican Treasury bills. Up to 10 percent of the fund's assets can be invested in Canadian government bills, with the balance in U.S. government-guaranteed securities. The fund yielded 7.6 percent through 1993.

VOLATILITY: THERE'S LESS THAN YOU'D THINK

Many investors think that currencies are volatile. Not true. Stock prices jump around much more than exchange rates. Generally, major currencies move up or down only 12 percent annually. The Canadian dollar's volatility is the lowest of any of the major currencies; it moves only half that much. The yen was 1993's exception, soaring 17 percent in the first half of the year, until the demise of the Liberal Democratic Party (which ruled Japanese politics for 38 years) stopped the yen from breaching the 100-yen-per-dollar level. Even the yen, though, was tame compared to stocks. Plenty of $40 stocks move 10 to 20 percent each month! While the S&P 500 Index is less volatile than individual stocks, it is usually at least twice as volatile as major currencies, *including currencies that devalue*.

THE GLOBAL INTERBANK MARKET

Banks throughout the world maintain extensive currency trading operations to handle the demands of their commercial and investment clients, and, more than ever, to buy and sell for their own profit. London, Frankfurt, Hong Kong, Tokyo, and Singapore are major foreign exchange trading centers. Practically all the large New York banks have departments devoted to currency trading, as do major banks in Los Angeles, Chicago, San Francisco, Detroit, Boston, and other U.S. cities.

Banks buy from and sell to one another, without regard to borders, directly by phone, telex, through brokers, and via computerized dealing networks. The market operates around the clock. West Coast banks trade through the opening of the Australian and the Far East markets; when Asian markets close, the Middle East is going strong and Europe's trading day opens. By the time the New York market starts, it's lunchtime in Europe. Chicago traders arrive between 6:30 A.M. and 7:00 A.M., their time, to start trading in the Interbank Market, but also because the International Monetary Market's

(IMM) currency futures exchange begins trading at 7:20 A.M. Chicago time. The early shift of West Coast currency traders are in the office by 6:00 A.M. their time and can trade with most foreign centers, at least briefly, during their day.

HOW TO READ CURRENCY QUOTES

The exchange rates for currencies you are considering buying are listed daily in major newspapers and weekly in *Barron's* and other financial publications. The global currency market has no official close, but U.S. papers typically list the midpoint between the bank market's buy and sell rates at 3:00 P.M. eastern time, toward the end of the active trading day in North America.

The list of exchange rates is brief compared with the number of stock quotes in the paper, yet the currency market is much larger. Over $1 trillion worth of currencies are traded daily.

The table below shows a listing of exchange rates from a Saturday paper. The prices in the first two columns are Thursday's and Friday's rate in dollars. One hundred British pounds cost $150.07 Friday versus $151.03 Thursday, and so on. Each row in the third and fourth column is how many British pounds, Canadian dollars, and so on it took on those days to buy one dollar.

4

THE FEDERAL RESERVE'S NOON RATES

Every day at noon, our Federal Reserve surveys the Interbank Market to determine how banks are pricing a dozen or so currencies. The Fed's "Noon Buying Rates" are the result. For an update on exchange rates, call the Federal Reserve at (212) 720-6693 to hear a recorded message of its Noon Foreign Exchange rates.

5
HOW CURRENCIES ARE QUOTED

	Foreign Currency in Dollars		The Dollar in Foreign Currency	
	Thursday	Friday	Thursday	Friday
Britain (pound)	1.5103	1.5007	.6621	.6664
Canada (dollar)	.7819	.7816	1.2790	1.2795
France (franc)	.1718	.1702	5.8210	5.8750
Germany (mark)	.5863	.5821	1.7055	1.7180
Japan (yen)	.009394	.009372	106.45	106.70
Mexico (new peso)	.3203	.3203	3.1220	3.1220
Switzerland (franc)	.6656	.6590	1.5023	1.5175

Note: To get a foreign currency—dollar quote from a dollar—foreign currency quote, simply take the inverse of the former. For example, let's take Thursday's dollar—Swiss rate of U.S. $1.00 = S.F. 1.5023. To find out how much one Swiss franc is worth, divide 1 by 1.5023 (1/1.5023), which is .6656, so S.F. 1.00 = U.S. $.6656.

FACTORS AFFECTING CURRENCY INVESTMENTS

These days, it's easy to get lost and drown in mounds of data. The three factors described below are looked at by professionals and knowledgeable investors alike.

FACTOR 1: PURCHASING POWER PARITY

Currencies have value based on the goods they can buy. When considering a currency for investment it is essential to know how its purchasing power compares to the dollar's. Over time, the dollar's exchange rate reflects its buying power in the United States compared with what another currency buys in its country. This is "Purchasing Power Parity" ("PPP"), the premise of which is that long-run currency price equilibrium occurs at the exchange rate where a basket of similar goods costs the same in either currency. It's a way of taking into account the fact that if we can get more for our money across the border we're going to get it (either directly ourselves, or via an importer who perceives the price disparity and goes and gets it for us). PPP takes into account the effect of millions of different international buying decisions; Canadian drivers cross the border to buy U.S. gas when they can get more gas for their money than in their own country; Texans cross into Mexico to purchase cheaper prescription drugs. Each involves a currency transaction that either increases the demand for U.S. dollars (as when Canadian drivers sell their currency for ours) or adds to the supply of U.S. dollars (as when a Texan sells U.S. dollars for pesos).

In practice currencies trade at a premium to or discount from their Purchasing Power Parity with the dollar. Since 1971 the Japanese yen has ranged from being 40 percent undervalued to being more than 30 percent overvalued against the dollar. Investors should watch for currencies that are undervalued on a PPP basis; such currencies are candidates for investment.

6

PURCHASING POWER PARITY

Following are exchange rates at which it is estimated that the purchasing power of the U.S. dollar is equivalent to the foreign currency.

	Exchange Rate as Measured by PPP$	Actual Rate as of May 1994	% Over- or Undervalued
British pound	1.53	1.49	- 2.5
Canadian dollar	.78	.72	- 8.3
German mark	.53	.60	+11.7
Japanese yen	.0075	.0098	+23.5
Swiss franc	.61	.71	+14.1

Only the Canadian dollar was sufficiently undervalued to consider investing in it. The dollar, in fact, had overshot its Purchasing Power Parity with the Japanese yen, German mark, and Swiss franc by mid-1994. Remember, however, PPP is a *long-run* measure of equilibrium, and, as such, is not a reliable investment indicator by itself. Currency exchange rates can remain over- or undervalued for months, even years at a time.

FACTOR 2: ECONOMIC DATA—ANALYZE COUNTRIES LIKE STOCKS

The press often refers to countries as if they were corporations—"Japan Inc.," "Corporate America," "the German Export Miracle." It can actually be profitable (and fun) to analyze countries as you would stocks, with currency rates as their prices. True, those countries would be massive conglomerates, but each would have different growth rates, competitiveness, and international profitability. Would you rather "own" a 3 percent or a 1 percent GDP growth rate? An improving trade balance? Political stability or chaos? As with a stock investment, you are better off investing in the currency of a country that is growing faster than its peers, is improving profitability, and has stable "management."

Use information that is in our Country Spotlights (Part 4), and which comes regularly across the pages of *Barron's*, the *Wall Street Journal*, and other financial papers, to rank which of the world's major economies is at the top of the heap and which is on the bottom.

GDP Growth

Economic growth is a country's equivalent of a company's total earnings before expenses. Rising growth in a country's Gross Domestic Product (GDP) is a plus for the currency, so long as the country does not take in an excess of imports during the process (and so hurt its trade balance). Is the trend in GDP up or down? As with stocks, we are more concerned with future earnings than past earnings. In 1993, the U.S. economy expanded while the German GDP declined, helping the dollar rise against the mark.

Interest Rates

A currency that pays high interest is attractive as an investment, but it invites inspection as well. Investors prefer higher interest rates as long as they don't stifle GDP growth. In 1993 traders bought the British pound over the German mark. U.K. interest rates were lower, but investors thought that high German rates (in other words, the high cost of German money) would stifle growth. They were right: The pound strengthened 7 percent against the D-mark in 1993.

Political Leadership

Who's running the place? How do the citizens think their leader is doing? Consider how a nation rates its leader as similar to how stockholders view the quality of a company's management. A low approval rating can mean inertia and uncertainty, which can have a negative impact on a currency. Will the leader's policies help the economy and make the country more competitive internationally? Does the government have a currency target? President Clinton's team did for the yen in 1993. The market went along and the dollar dropped almost 20 percent in the first half of 1993. Investors prefer political stability, which promotes economic growth. If investors lose confidence in the stability of an economy, that country's currency will reflect this lack of faith by falling in value.

Balance of Payments

Is the current account in surplus or deficit? A country's current account measures whether it is a net seller of goods and services to the rest of the world or is a net buyer. The current account includes the "Trade Balance" in manufactured goods, as well as the so-called "Services Balance," which comprises net receipts in such areas as tourism, earnings on foreign investments, and overseas insurance and banking fees. The U.S. current account is in deficit, but less so than our trade balance because we run a surplus in services.

If our deficit with Japan deteriorates further, the yen will continue to gain. Remember, however, that the United States' current account is affected by the economic growth rate of countries that are U.S. customers. In 1995, as GDP growth in Germany and Japan increases, there should be increased demand for U.S. exports, and the U.S. current account should improve.

DM Monthly Chart

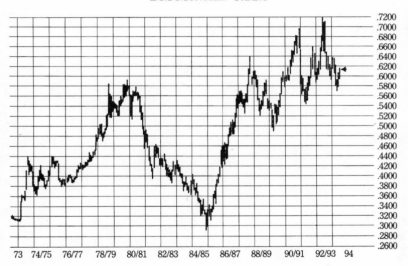

73   74/75   76/77   78/79   80/81   82/83   84/85   86/87   88/89   90/91   92/93   94

The German mark has followed several multi-year trends during the last 20 years. Since 1989 the mark has had trends lasting 6 months to two years.

Factor 3: Market Momentum

Currency prices are propelled higher, on balance, when an uptrend is in place. They are pushed lower in the presence of a downtrend. Second, it is easier to make money when you are buying in an uptrend, because demand for the currency is outstripping supply. It even feels easier—as does swimming with the current. The opposite also holds true. Swimming against the tide makes it hard to keep your head above water.

How do we find an uptrend? There is a simple indicator which can serve the currency investor well. It turns bullish when a currency's price begins trading above its average price of the past fifty-two weeks (in other words, one year). This fifty-two-week moving average is a simple on-off indicator, either bullish or bearish. Since it is derived strictly from a history of currency prices, it is "dispassionate." You need a signal devoid of emotion in markets that can appear most bullish or bearish right before they change direction.

CD WEEKLY CHART

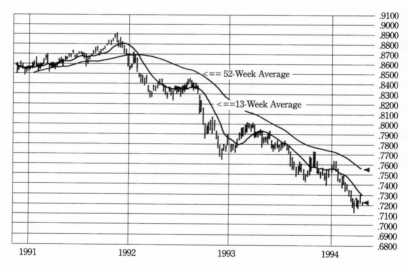

The Canadian dollar has closed each week's trading below its 52-week moving average since late 1991. Look for that trend to change. As of August 1994, the Canadian dollar was undervalued compared to the U.S. dollar on a Purchasing Power Parity Basis, and Canada ranked first on our Currency Picklist. Odds are that the Canadian dollar will trade above its 52-week moving average in late 1994 or early 1995, despite an expected referendum on Quebec independence, and rise further from there.

Most brokers and bankers can bring this data up on their computer screen in less than a minute. Ask them to fax you a copy. The fifty-two-week average is a long-term price line that is rarely crossed, but if a currency closes the week above that line, there is a high probability of a sustained uptrend. On the Canadian dollar weekly chart on page 224 I have superimposed a fifty-two-week moving average of the Canadian dollar's price over a weekly chart of the Canadian currency. Each line on the chart shows the high, low, and closing price for a given week. I also superimposed a thirteen-week (three-month) moving average, which is particularly useful in timing when to sell a currency investment. When this average crosses above the fifty-two-week average (see chart), it is confirmation that a currency is in an uptrend.

Ways to Invest

Foreign Currency CDs

You can purchase foreign currency certificates of deposit from the private banking departments of national and regional banks. If the bank is federally chartered, its CDs can be FDIC insured. For instance:

Citibank's Private Banking Division, New York, NY. Phone: (212) 559-5959. Minimum investment: $25,000.

One bank that specializes in foreign currency CDs, also FDIC insured, is:

Mark Twain Bank, St. Louis, MO. Phone: (800) 926-4922. Minimum investment: $20,000.

Money Market Deposit Accounts

Some banks offer U.S.-based interest-bearing deposit accounts in foreign currencies. Money can be withdrawn at any time. For this convenience you may receive a slightly lower interest rate. One such bank is:

Credit Suisse, Private Banking, New York, NY. Phone: (212) 238-2000. Minimum investment: $20,000.

FOREIGN CURRENCY MONEY MARKET FUNDS

Some mutual-fund companies offer foreign currency money market funds. Fidelity Investments runs three separate funds in Japanese yen, German marks, and British pounds. An advantage is that *you invest with U.S. dollars*, at a dollar share price, the same as you would with mutual funds. Although there is a 0.40 percent sales fee, the currency funds earn higher rates of interest than on CD's or deposit accounts. Their share prices are quoted daily.

Fidelity Investments, Boston, MA. Phone: (800) 544-8888. Minimum investment: $3,000.

CURRENCY MUTUAL FUNDS

Franklin Funds offers three funds—Hard Currency, High Income Currency, and Global Currency—with professional managers who decide when to invest U.S. dollars in a variety of foreign currencies.

Franklin Funds: (800) 342-5436.

THE INTERBANK MARKET

Currency markets are unregulated. Because there is no equivalent of a Securities and Exchange Commission (SEC), investors are cautioned against buying currency by themselves from the Interbank Market. If you do, don't be shy about asking in advance how the currencies are priced. The best currency rate is the "interbank rate" (the rate at which banks buy and sell to each other). Are you getting the interbank rate? Even if your bank has a currency trading department, it may not be set up to service currency investors. Avoid banks that cannot clearly explain their currency pricing policy. You wouldn't buy a stock without having a good idea of the price you'll pay.

Warning: Do not make a currency investment without knowing the exchange rate being used to convert your dollars.

There is no rulebook; one bank might charge $50 to transact a $20,000 currency trade while another might charge $250.

1995'S CURRENCY INVESTMENT CANDIDATE

Watch the Canadian dollar. It is undervalued on a Purchasing Power Parity basis. Its economy is expanding faster than ours. Its interest rates are higher *and* its inflation is lower. As of mid-1994, the Canadian dollar was not trading above its fifty-two-week moving average of $0.7548; wait to invest in the Canadian currency until market momentum is pushing it higher. Then all three of our investment factors will be bullish for that currency, and odds will favor the Canadian dollar rising in value against the U.S. dollar.

Hint: Everything's Relative With Currencies

For the Canadian dollar to go up against the U.S. dollar, news from Canada does not have to be good, it just needs to be better than news for the U.S. dollar.

CHAPTER THIRTEEN

BEYOND NAFTA

After three years of gritty negotiation and debate, the North American Free Trade Agreement (NAFTA) was approved by the U.S. Congress in 1993. The last time Mexico received so much attention from the United States was during the Mexican–American War of 1847. NAFTA assures free trade among the United States, Canada, and Mexico. The ramifications of this agreement are far-reaching, but here we will focus on the impact for investors, which boils down to one simple fact—that

> NAFTA creates a huge free-trade market of more than 300 million customers and clients for U.S. products and services, for Mexican products and services, and for Canadian products and services.

The greatest impact of NAFTA, of course, will be felt by Mexico. The country's GDP, at $320 billion, represents only about 5 percent of the U.S. GDP, and NAFTA could add 15 percent additional GDP growth to the Mexican economy over a ten-year period. This compares with a total 1 percent additional gain to U.S. growth over the same time period.

Mexico's population, unlike the United States', is largely young and growing; it is also one that has a low standard of living compared with ours. NAFTA will help Mexico develop faster as a market and at the same time raise its standard of living and disposable-income level. The agreement gives U.S. and Canadian companies "privileged" access to this young and growing population with ability to sell to Mexican consumers in the same way they now sell to consumers in Miami, Montreal, Maui, and Memphis, without tariffs or quotas—that, in essence, is the power of free trade.

NAFTA also sends a positive signal to all of Latin America, indicating that the United States will want stronger trade relations with Argentina and Chile. Likewise, the agreement also encourages Peru, Brazil, and Venezuela to continue with their economic reforms, just as Mexico has done. (*Note*: Prior to NAFTA, Mexico had lowered its inflation rate, slashed its foreign debt, reduced its budget surplus, and raised wages. See Mexico in Chapter 11 for details.) As these other countries follow Mexico's example, investment opportunities will arise. Read the country watch sections on these Latin American countries for background information.

How to Profit from NAFTA

Certain industries are logical beneficiaries of NAFTA: banking, infrastructure, telecommunications, transportation, building and cement, pharmaceuticals, and personal care. Within these (or other) industries, you can invest in (1) stocks of U.S. companies that already have a large presence in Mexico and/or whose products and services will be purchased by Mexicans; (2) stocks of Mexican companies that will see increased business as the country's standard of living rises and consumers have more disposable income; and (3) open- and closed-end mutual funds specializing in Mexican securities.

If you decide to buy shares of Mexican stocks, bear in mind the warning issued by the country's president, Carlos Salinas, when the treaty was passed: "For the first time ever, Mexico has a deadline for becoming more efficient. There is no more *mañana*." In other words, although the phaseout of North American tariffs gives a huge boost to Mexico's economy and its self-esteem, it also puts the country's inefficient industries directly in competition with more experienced U.S. and Canadian corporations. This is almost certain to hurt some Mexican companies, most particularly small textile makers, manufacturers, and farmers. Even local banks are going to be under the gun: NAFTA allows U.S. and Canadian banks to set up subsidiaries in Mexico. And, small retailers could be flattened by the huge Mexican chains, such as **Cifra** and **El Puerto de Liverpool**, which have formed joint ventures with **WalMart** and **K mart**. The bottom line: Avoid Mexican companies that are not up to speed—that have not invested in new technology and worker training—as they are unlikely to be competitive with U.S. and Canadian conglomerates that produce more efficiently.

U.S. STOCKS

In anticipation of NAFTA, many U.S. corporations, including **Bell Atlantic Corp.**, **Coca-Cola**, **PepsiCo**, and **Colgate-Palmolive**, had already increased their presence in Mexico. The expectation is that these and other large publicly traded corporations will see rising revenues as NAFTA settles into place. (See Chapter 4 on Multinationals.) Under the agreement, Mexico will immediately halve its 20 percent tariff on autos imported from the United States and Canada and eliminate it entirely over the next ten years. In return, the United States will abolish its 2.5 percent tariff on imported Mexican cars.

The pent-up demand for cars is likely to benefit **Chrysler**, **General Motors**, and, similarly, Superior Industries, a leading maker of original equipment cast aluminum wheels, which is opening a plant in Mexico in late 1994.

The need and desire to talk on the phone is enormous in any emerging market, and nowhere is it greater than in Mexico. One American company already well established in this field in Mexico is **Southwestern Bell** which has a 10 percent stake in **Telefonos de Mexico**, Mexico's national telephone system. And the cellular business, which has been a large profit center for **Southwestern Bell**, is yet another area the company can expand across the border.

Owning one's own phone is just the tip of the iceberg. As the country becomes more sophisticated, fax machines, modems, and cellular phones will be in demand. In addition to Southwestern Bell and ADRs of Telefonos de Mexico, another choice is **Mobile Telecommunications Technology**, a leading provider of paging services. It operates in both Mexico and Canada, providing subscribers with seamless roaming services throughout North America.

Burlington Northern stands to benefit from reduction of transportation restrictions brought about by NAFTA and the subsequent increased need to ship products. The company has an advantage in that it is headquartered near the Mexican border in Fort Worth, Texas.

R. R. Donnelley & Sons has acquired Laboratorio Lito Color, a printer with operations in Mexico City and San Juan del Rio and is now doubling the size of the San Juan operation.

Gerber Products is already the leader in baby foods in Mexico. The strength and appeal of the Gerber brand name reaches throughout the country, and the company is expanding its production facilities and distributon reach.

Kimberly-Clark, anticipating this rapidly developing market, owns 43 percent of Kimberly-Clark de Mexico, one of the country's leading consumer products companies. Growth has been in the double digits.

Rubbermaid has officially stated its aim to derive 25 percent of its business from overseas by the year 2000, up from about 15 percent in 1993. As part of its goal, the company has widened its Mexican exposure with the acquisition of CIPSA, the leading plastics and rubber housewares product company in Mexico. Rubbermaid also has a sizeable position in Canada. Its recycling-products division is experiencing phenomenal growth in both domestic and foreign markets. The company has reported fifty quarters of consecutively higher earnings.

WalMart Stores has a joint venture with Cifra, Mexico's largest retailer, to open wholesale club stores and in fact has already opened its first two units. Another way to "play" the growing retail market is through **Sears, Roebuck.**

MEXICAN STOCKS

A number of Mexican companies are expected to see greater demand for their products and services as the result of not only NAFTA but also of the country's impressive ongoing economic reforms and rising incomes.

- **Cemex** (DMXBY: ADR)
  Mexico's premier cement maker should be busy meeting the huge demand for for infrastructure construction, particularly for new highways, railroads, airports, electric and water plants, airports, hospitals, and schools.

- **Coca-Cola Gemsa** (NYSE: KOF)
  A new joint venture between the U.S. company Coca-Cola and one of Mexico's leading producers of beer. Both have popular products that are expected to do well on both sides of the border.

- **Grupo Carso** (OTC: GPOAF)
  As the largest auto parts manufacturer in Mexico, the company should profit in the near term from the agreement.

- **Grupo DINA** (NYSE: DIN)
  This company will start to import components, primarily engines, from the United States on a duty-free basis while continuing to enjoy tariff protection on its finished trucks for a ten-year period.

- **Maseca** (NASDAQ: GIMBY)
  This $456 million company, which makes corn flour, operates more efficiently than many. It has raised its share of Mexico's tortilla market from about 55 percent in 1988 to more than 70 percent in 1994.

- **Telefonos de Mexico** (NYSE: TMX ADRs)
  International and domestic long-distance calls are
  expected to soar. Shares in the national phone com-
  pany are a logical choice.
- **Televisa** (NASDAQ: GRTVY)
  This is Mexico's leading commercial TV and cable
  network ($1.4 billion). It also owns the world's largest
  Spanish-language video library.
- **Transportacion Maritima Mexicana** (NYSE:
  TMM)
  This shipping company could have a substantial surge
  in both its sea and land transportation business.

BANKING ON MEXICO

There's been much press about the fact that Mexican certificates of deposit pay tantalizingly higher rates than do CDs
sold by U.S. banks. However, unlike U.S. CDs, which are
insured up to $100,000 by the FDIC, the Mexican variety is
not, although the Mexican government has never allowed a
bank to fail.

A safer option with a lot less red tape: Invest in a mutual
fund that holds Mexican debt. Here are four to consider:

- Fidelity's relatively new **New Markets Income
  Fund** has about 40 percent of its portfolio in Mexican
  bonds or money markets. Phone: (800) 544-8888.
- Franklin Funds' **High Income Currency Portfolio**
  can invest up to 5 percent of its assets in the money
  market funds of a minor currency country, such as
  Mexico. Phone: (800) 354- 4111.

- Scudder's closed-end **Latin America Dollar Income Fund** invests heavily in Mexican bonds and money markets. Phone: (800) 225-2470.

- T. C. West's **North American Money Trust** can invest 20 percent of its portfolio in Mexican short-term paper and 20 percent in Canadian short-term paper. Phone: (800) 869-3863 or (800) 526-3143.

VI

APPENDIX

1
Foreign Currency Bank Accounts

Up until recently, U.S. residents who wanted to trade foreign currencies had to open a foreign bank account or buy currencies from a U.S. dealer. Beginning in 1990, however, the Federal Reserve Board ruled that U.S. banks could offer customers foreign currency accounts. Only a few do. *Caution*: Although these accounts are protected by federal deposit insurance, up to $100,000 each, they are not protected from losses due to currency swings.

Citibank
Product Sales Center
580 White Plains Rd.
Tarrytown, NY 10591
(800) 321-2484

Accounts in British pounds, Canadian dollars, German D-marks, Japanese yen, and Swiss francs. Minimum deposit: $25,000.

Available as time deposits (3, 6, 9 months) and as multicurrency money market accounts.

First Union National Bank of North Carolina
1 First Union Center
Foreign Exchange Dept.
Charlotte, NC 28288
(800) 736-5636

Accounts in Australian dollars, British pounds, Canadian dollars, French francs, German D-marks, Italian lira, Japanese yen, and Swiss francs. Minimum deposit: $100,000.

Mark Twain Bank
1630 South Lindbergh Blvd.
St. Louis, MO 63131
(800) 926-4922; (314) 997-9208

Accounts in all major foreign currencies (about twenty-five). Minimum investment: $20,000

2
Buying Individual Foreign Stocks and Bonds

If you're itching to buy and sell foreign stocks that are not traded on the American exchanges or over the counter, check first with your stockbroker, bearing in mind that few U.S. brokers handle retail orders for foreign stocks. Or, call one of the firms listed below. Merrill Lynch, for example, will buy stocks anywhere it has a branch office—it has them in more than thirty countries, with branches in Frankfurt, Hong Kong, London, Paris, and Tokyo, among others. Minimum investments vary among firms, depending upon whether or not you already have an account with the firm, the country involved, and the price of the shares. Most firms require a minimum trade of at least $25,000. As we go to press, the discount brokers we contacted were not handling foreign stocks, but that is likely to change.

- Bear Stearns
- PaineWebber
- Merrill Lynch
- Smith Barney Shearson

Other factors to consider:

1) Some foreign markets levy fees and taxes on trades, generally adding to the price you pay but reducing your capital gains.

2) Settlement is often slow, anywhere from a week to a month.

3) Securities Investor Protection Corp. (SIPC) insurance covers only stock purchased through and held by a U.S. brokerage firm that is already a member of SIPC. SIPC insures up to $500,000 per account against losses if the firm becomes insolvent. *Caution*: If you trade through a non-U.S. broker, you could lose your entire investment if that broker declares bankruptcy.

4) Foreign brokers, unlike their U.S. counterparts, do not report to the IRS annual dividend income and gains from securities sold. Therefore, you must do your own record keeping.

5) If you invest in a country that withholds taxes on dividends you earn then you must file IRS Form 1116 to claim a foreign tax credit.

3
Your Information Library

Most publications dealing with international markets are expensive. We suggest that before subscribing you read one or two issues at your public library or call for a free sample. Our favorites are listed below.

GENERAL READING

Asian Wall Street Journal Weekly	(800) 568-7625
Business Week	(800) 635-1200
The Economist	(800) 456-6086
Financial Times (London)	(800) 628-8088
Forbes	(800) 888-9896
International Herald-Tribune	(800) 882-2884
Investor's Business Daily	(800) 992-2126
New York Times	(800) 631-2500
Wall Street Journal	(800) 568-7625

TRACKING MUTUAL FUNDS

Value Line Mutual Fund Survey
Biweekly: $295/year
3 months: $49
711 Third Avenue
New York, NY 10017
(800) 284-7607, ext. 8409

Analysis of 1,500 funds plus less detailed information on 500 others; ranks funds from 1 (worst) to 5 (best); does not review any of Value Line's own mutual funds.

Morningstar Mutual Funds
Biweekly: $395/year
3 months: $55
225 West Wacker Drive
Chicago, IL 60606
(800) 876-5005

Ranks funds by star system; compares each fund's total return (net asset value plus dividends and capital gains) against the return of all international stock markets, against all mutual funds, and then against all mutual funds with the same investment objectives.

Morningstar Closed-end Funds
Biweekly: $195/year
3 months: $35
see above for address and telephone number

Limited Supply Securities
David Schachter
905 Hewlett Dr.
North Woodmere, NY 11591

(516) 791-4444

Free brochure listing phone numbers for closed-end funds; automated quote service for equity and country funds.

PERIODICALS LISTING MUTUAL FUND PERFORMANCE FIGURES

Barron's Weekly	(800) 544-0422
Forbes Magazine	(800) 888-9896
Kiplinger's Personal Finance	(800) 544-0155
Money	(800) 633-9970
Your Money	(800) 777-0025

TRACKING ADRs AND MULTINATIONAL AND FOREIGN STOCKS

Value Line Investment Survey
Weekly: $525/year
10 weeks: $55
711 Third Avenue
New York, NY 10017
(800) 284-7606

Covers the leading ADRs and ranks them for safety and timeliness. Helpful in analyzing the multinationals; gives the percentage of revenues derived from foreign operations or sales to foreign countries.

The Outlook
Weekly: $289/year
Standard & Poor's Corp.
25 Broadway
New York, NY 10005
(212) 208-8000; (800) 221-5277

Frequently analyzes ADRs, stocks of multinational corporations, and foreign equity and bond mutual funds.

Research Reports
$10/report
Standard & Poor's Corp.
25 Broadway
New York, NY 10005
(800) 642-2858

Analysis, ratings, earnings estimates, and historical data on more than 4,000 publicly traded companies, including ADRs and multinationals. Gathered from some 2,000 Wall Street analysts at 150 contributing firms. Updated daily. Includes a buy/hold/sell recommendation.

Moody's International Manual & News Reports
Weekly: $2,495/year
Moody's Investors Service
99 Church Street
New York, NY 10007
(212) 553-0300; (800) 342-5647

Three-volume annual containing financial information on more than 7,500 companies and institutions in 100 countries.

NEWSLETTERS

Capital International Perspective
Monthly: $6,000/year
Morgan Stanley
1251 Avenue of the Americas
New York, NY 10020
(212) 703-2964

Analyzes the performance records of more than 2,500 companies around the world.

The International Bank Credit Analyst
Monthly: $695/year
BCA Publications
3463 Peel Street
Montreal, Quebec H3A 1W7
Canada
(514) 398-0653

Analyzes interest rates, economic trends, currency swings, and gold and commodity prices around the world.

International Economic Conditions
Quarterly: free
Research & Public Information Division

Federal Reserve Bank of St. Louis
P.O. Box 442
St. Louis, MO 63166
(314) 444-8809

Charts, graphs, and commentary on economic situations around the world; easy to understand.

Pring Market Review
Monthly: $395/year
International Institute for Economic Research
Martin J. Pring, Editor
P.O. Box 624
Gloucester, VA 23061
(804) 694-0415

Covers world financial markets, using graphs and technical analysis; includes foreign stock markets, debt markets, currencies, precious metals.

John Dessaur's Investors World
Monthly: $99/year
P.O. Box 1718
Orleans, MA 02653
(508) 255-1651

Covers major markets and recommends appropriate individual securities and investment strategies; tracks performance of recommended investments each month.

Investor's Guide to Closed-End Funds
Monthly: $325/year
Herzfeld Publications
Box 161465
Miami, FL 33116
(800) 854-3863; (305) 271-1900

Gives sample portfolios and recommends individual single-country funds.

Frank Cappiello's Closed-End Fund Digest
Monthly: $200/year
1224 Coast Village Circle
Suite 11
Santa Barbara, CA 93108
(800) 282-2335

Covers all closed-end funds, giving their performance results by categories; with recommended model portfolios.

OTHER PUBLICATIONS

The Basics of Foreign Trade and Exchange
free
Public Information
Federal Reserve Bank of New York
33 Liberty Street
New York, NY 10045
(212) 720-6134

A forty-eight-page booklet, written for students of business and economics and those in corporate training programs, that explains competitiveness in global markets, the Federal Reserve's role, and trade issues.

Foreign Exchange Markets in the United States
by Roger M. Kubarych.
$2 from:
Federal Reserve Bank of New York (see above)

A twenty-plus-page pamphlet that gives the fundamentals, in easy-to-understand language.

The World Gold Council
900 Third Avenue (26th floor)
New York, NY 10022
(212) 688-0005

Call for listing of books and pamphlets on gold.

COMPUTERIZED INFORMATION

Dow Jones News Retrieval
P.O. Box 300
Princeton, NJ 08543–0300
(800) 522-3567

On-line data with more than sixty different financial bases; includes news, quotes, research.

Standard & Poor's MarketScope Europe
Standard & Poor's ComStock
600 Mamaroneck Avenue
Harrison, NY 10528
(800) 431-5019

Available over Reuters and S&P ComStock, or by direct delivery from S&P; based in London. Analysts and journalists report on foreign investment ideas, research recommendations, financial news, corporate data, and forecasts. Includes a database with fundamental and forecast data for more than 2,500 European companies.

4
A List of Foreign Currencies

Argentinean austral
Austrian schilling
Australian dollar
Bahrain dinar
Belgian franc
Bolivian boliviano
Brazilian cruzado
British pound
Canadian dollar
Chilean peso
Chinese yuan
Colombian peso
Cuban peso
Danish krone
Djbouti franc
Dutch guilder
Ecuadorian sucre
Ethiopian birr
Finnish markka
French franc
German D-mark
Ghanaian cedi
Greek drachma
Hong Kong dollar
Icelandic krona
Indian rupee
Indonesian rupiah
Iranian rial
Irish pound
Israeli shekel
Italian lira
Japanese yen
Korean won
Kuwaiti dinar
Laotian kip

Lebanese pound
Libyan dinar
Luxembourg franc
Malaysian ringgit
Maltese lira
Mexican peso
Mongolian tugrik
Mozambique meticai
Netherlands: see *Dutch*
New Zealand dollar
Nicaraguan cordoba
Norwegian krone
Peruvian inti
Philippine peso
Polish zloti
Portuguese escudo
Russian ruble
Saudi Arabian riyal
Sierra Leonean leone
Singapore dollar
Somalian shilling
South African rand
Spanish peseta
Swedish krona
Swiss franc
Taiwanese dollar
Thailand baht
Turkish lira
Ugandan shilling
United Arab Emirate dirham
Uruguayan peso
Venezuelan bolivar
Vietnamese dong
Zairian zaire
Zambian kwacha

5

A Foreign Baedeker: Investment Jargon Made Simple

ADR:
American Depositary Receipt; a document indicating ownership of shares of a foreign stock; ADRs trade in dollars on the U.S. stock exchanges or over the counter.

Appreciation:
Growth in the value of an asset.

Arbitrage:
Benefiting from differences in price of the same commodity, currency, or security traded on two or more markets. An arbitrageur makes money by selling in one market and simultaneously buying in another.

Average Annual Return:
The total return from an investment, including capital gains or losses plus dividends and interest income; expressed as an average annual percentage.

Basis Point:
A measure used to determine moves in bond yields. A basis point equals 0.01, or one-hundredth of one percent. If a bond's yield moves from 6 to 7 percent, it's increased one hundred basis points.

Bear Market:
Time period during which stocks keep falling in value or stay at depressed prices.

Big Bang:
October 27, 1986, when the London Stock Exchange ended fixed brokerage commissions.

Bond:
A long-term debt security, issued by corporations, municipalities, and the government that pays regular interest to the investor. The bondholder has rights to receive interest and return of principal but no ownership in the issuing corporation.

Bottom Up:
Method of selecting securities used by portfolio managers that focuses on buying good stocks, based on their fundamental values,

regardless of what is taking place in the stock market or the economy at large.

Bourse:
French word for stock exchange (from "purse"). Also used by exchanges in Switzerland and Belgium.

Brady Bond:
Named for former Treasury Secretary Nicholas Brady, these bonds are issued by foreign countries such as Mexico, Nigeria, and Venezuela. Most are dollar denominated, and their principal is almost always backed by U.S. Treasury bonds, which reduces their risk level.

Bullion:
Refined gold or silver in bulk (i.e., ingots) rather than in the form of coins. Central banks hold their gold in bars or ingots.

Bull Market:
Time period during which stocks keep rising in price.

Call:
A bond provision allowing the issuer to recall the bond before maturity. Issuers recall bonds when it's to their advantage to retire older issues that have high interest rates and replace them with new issues at lower rates.

Capital Gain:
Profit due to the rise in value of stocks, bonds, or other securities. Long-term gains are the result of securities held more than one year; short-term gains are the result of sales of securities held one year or less.

Capital Gains Distributions:
Payments made by mutual funds to shareholders, usually in December, of long-term capital gains achieved by selling securities held by the fund.

Closed-end Investment Company:
A mutual fund that issues a set number of shares and then trades on one of the stock exchanges or over the counter.

Current Yield:
Dividends paid to investors; stated as a percentage of the investment's current price.

Custodian:
Bank or other financial institution that holds stock certificates, bonds, or other assets for safekeeping.

Denationalization:
When a government-owned corporation is turned over to private ownership.

Distributions:
Payments made by a mutual fund to shareholders, derived from the sale of the fund's securities, from interest income and/or dividends.

Diversification:
An investment approach that spreads one's money over a number of different investments or securities in order to reduce risk so that poor performance by one security will not have an overwhelming impact on the portfolio.

Dividends:
Money that a company pays the owners of its stocks, typically four times a year; dividends can sometimes be in the form of additional stock instead of cash.

Dow Jones Industrial Average:
The most popular price-weighted market indicator. The DJIA consists of thirty actively traded blue-chip stocks that represent the stock market as a whole; their price movement is a used as a benchmark or measurement of the stock market.

ECU:
European currency unit, developed by nations of the European Common Market. Consists of a weighted basket of European currencies. In 1992 it became the unit of account for the Common Market as well as the currency in which all EC bonds, CDs, and other loans are traded. Included are the Belgian franc, British pound, Danish krone, Dutch guilder, French franc, German D-mark, Greek drachma, Irish pound, Italian lira, Portuguese escudo, and Spanish peseta.

Equities:
Stocks, real estate, and other assets owned by investors as opposed to bonds in which investors lend money to the issuer.

Eurobond:
Debt issued in one European country's currency but sold outside that currency.

Face Value:
The value stated on the certificate of a bond, note, or other financial instrument. It is the amount for which the instrument will be redeemed upon maturity. Prior to maturity, the bond may trade in the secondary market above or below face value. Also called par value. Most bonds have a face value of $1,000.

Foreign Exchange Rate:
Price of one currency in terms of another.

1

The foreign exchange rate is the rate at which one country's currency is exhanged for another. Most often it is expressed as the number of foreign currency units per one U.S. dollar.

For example:

If $1.00 buys 1.6 German D-marks, the exchange rate is 1.6.

Or, it can be expressed in terms of the dollar value of one foreign currency unit.

For example:

The value of one mark is $0.63.

Forward Contract:
A contract to deliver a commodity, security, or currency at a specified rate at a specified time in the future.

Front-end Load:
Sales commission that investors pay when they purchase shares of a mutual fund.

Futures Contract:
A contract providing for the exchange of a financial asset or commodity at an agreed-upon price in a future month. This contract obligates the seller to sell and the buyer to buy at the predetermined price on the settlement date. (With an option, the buyer may elect to exercise the option, but with a futures contract the buyer is committed to fulfill the contract.)

Global Mutual Fund:
A fund that invests in U.S. and foreign stocks.

Gross Domestic Product:
(Formerly Gross National Product.) The sum total of a country's economic output; its goods and services, including the total value of its exports but not its imports.

Hedging:
Strategies used by mutual-fund managers to reduce risk; they buy or sell options or futures contracts to reduce the risk of holding another type of security.

Index:
A yardstick that measures changes in stock and bond prices. Major indexes: Dow Jones Industrial Average, Standard & Poor's 500.

Index Mutual Fund:
A fund that emulates an index, such as the Standard & Poor's 500. It invests in a basket of the equities that constitute the index. A stock index, for example, mirrors the performance of the S&P 500 or the U.K.'s FTSE-100 Share Index.

International Fund:
A fund that invests in foreign stocks. (See *Global Mutual Fund*.)

Junk Bonds:
Bonds rated BB or below by Standard & Poor's or Bb or below by Moody's; these bonds pay a higher yield than investment-grade bonds, which are considered much safer.

Liquidity:
Refers to how quickly and easily an asset can be converted to cash without substantially changing the price or value. For example, a checking account or money market fund is more liquid than a piece of real estate.

Load:
Commission or sales charge imposed by some mutual funds. The load or commission goes to the stockbroker or, in the case of low-load funds, to the fund itself.

Maturity:
The date when a bond (or loan) is due to be paid off and the bond-holder receives the principal amount (or face value) back.

Moving Average:
An average of security or commodity prices over a specific time period that shows the trend of prices. For example, a thirty-day

moving average includes yeterday's prices, and tomorrow it will include today's prices but will drop those for the earliest day included in the average. In other words, each day it picks up prices for the latest day while dropping those for the earliest day.

Net Asset Value:
The quoted price per share of a mutual fund; arrived at after the market closes each day by taking the value of the fund's holdings, subtracting its liabilities or debts (such as taxes owed), and dividing by the number of shares outstanding.

No-Load:
A mutual fund that does not charge an up-front sales charge. (Some "no load" funds do charge 12b-1 fees.)

Noon Buying Rate:
Average currency exchange rate as determined daily by the Federal Reserve Bank for the U.S. dollar vis-à-vis other currencies.

Open-end Investment Company:
A fund that continually issues new shares, thus increasing its net assets. The fund buys and sells shares directly to its customers.

Option:
A security that gives the right to purchase or sell a stated number of shares of a stock at a fixed price for a specified time.

Over the Counter:
The market in which securities are traded through dealers using telephones and a computerized network rather than on the floor of a stock exchange. The National Association of Securities Dealers (NASD) enforces the regulations. OTC stocks are almost always of smaller corporations.

Performance:
Tells how well (or poorly) a mutual fund has done over a given time period as measured by capital gains, dividends, and interest earned and presented as a percentage figure.

Pink Sheets:
Over-the-counter stocks that are not traded on the stock exchanges or in the NASDAQ listings. Instead, they are listed on pink sheets compiled daily by the National Quotations Bureau. The pink sheets list bid and asked prices and market makers.

Point:
A point indicates a $1 movement in the price of a stock; with a bond, a point is a 1 percent change in the par value of the bond.

Portfolio:
The securities owned by an individual, a mutual fund, bank, trust company, or fiduciary fund. Most portfolios comprise a variety of investments in order to reduce risk.

Portfolio Manager:
The person(s) making buy-and-sell decisions for a mutual fund.

Principal:
The amount of money one invests; the face value of a bond.

Prospectus:
Official, printed selling document describing a mutual fund's strategy, aim, risks, and costs; it must be given to potential investors. A preliminary prospectus is a red herring.

Purchasing Power of the Dollar:
Measure of the amount of goods and services that the dollar can buy in a particular market, compared with a prior time period.

Purchasing Power Parity:
The currency exchange rate at which a basket of similar goods in two different countries will cost the same in either currency.

Redemption Fee:
Fee a fund may charge if investors sell their shares before a stated time, ranging from thirty days to two years; ranges from 0.25 to 2 percent. Fee goes to the fund to pay for the transaction costs incurred by short-term traders.

Secondary Market:
The place where already issued stocks and bonds are traded after their initial public offering (IPO).

Securities:
Stocks, bonds, options, warrants.

SEC:
Securities and Exchange Commission; a federal agency created in 1934 that administers securities and mutual-fund laws and regulations.

Spread:
The difference between the bid and offer prices of a stock or bond.

Standard & Poor's 500:
A measure of stock market activity based on the prices of 500 widely owned common stocks—400 industrials, 40 financial, 40 public utility, and 20 transportation securities.

Stock:
Certificates representing ownership in a corporation.

Supernationals:
Agencies formed by groups of countries to help their economies, such as the International Monetary Fund and the World Bank.

Top Down:
Method of purchasing stocks used by portfolio managers that involves studying overall market and economic trends and then determining which companies and industries are likely to appreciate.

Total Return:
Total profit or loss that an investment returns to its investors over a stated time period; includes capital gains or losses, interest, and dividend income and expenses; expressed as a percentage of the original value of the assets.

12b-1 Fee:
Named after SEC Rule 12b-1; lets a mutual fund take part of its assets to pay for certain distribution and marketing costs; called a "hidden" load, it is deducted annually from investors' stake in the fund.

Underwriter:
Someone who purchases securities from an issuer for resale to the public.

Volatility:
Price changes in a security, mutual fund shares, currency, or an index of securities; can be used to measure an investment's risk.

Yankee Bond:
An international bond issued by a foreign bank or corporation but one that trades in U.S. dollars and is registered for sale in the United States.

Yield:
The dividends or interest income paid by a corporation or mutual fund; expressed as a percentage of the current stock price or, in the case of a fund, its share price; does not include capital gains or losses.

INDEX